ODDBALL COLORADO

ODDBALL COLORADO

A Guide to Some Really
STRANGE PLACES

JEROME POHLEN

CHICAGO
REVIEW
PRESS

Library of Congress Cataloging-in-Publication Data

Pohlen, Jerome.
  Oddball Colorado : a guide to some really strange places /
Jerome Pohlen.—1st ed.
    p. cm.
  Includes bibliographical references and indexes.
  ISBN 1-55652-460-9
  1. Colorado—Guidebooks. 2. Colorado—History, Local—Miscellanea.
  3. Curiosities and wonders—Colorado. I. Title
F774.3 .P64 2002
      917.8804'34—dc21

                              2002004122

Cover photo: Courtesy David "D. B." Cooper; artist and model, Lyle Nichols.

The author has made every effort to secure permissions for all the material in this book.
If any acknowledgment has inadvertently been omitted, please contact the author.

All photographs courtesy of Jerome Pohlen unless otherwise noted.
Cover and interior design: Mel Kupfer

Published by Chicago Review Press, Incorporated
814 North Franklin Street
Chicago, Illinois 60610
ISBN 1-55652-460-9
Printed in the United States of America
5 4 3 2 1

FOR MY GRANDMOTHER,
**VIRGINIA MAE
GREEN STANDIFORD,**
WHO WAS BORN
IN EAGLE, COLORADO.

Contents

INTRODUCTION

*H*ere's a news flash: Colorado is stunning. The state has breathtaking scenery, quaint vacation hideaways, and enough outdoor activities to choke a dude ranch horse. But let me ask you, when it comes to the great outdoors, hasn't it been done . . . or more accurately, *over*done? After all, there isn't just one majestic 14,000-foot peak to conquer in Colorado, there are 54! Yet how many high-altitude alligator farms are there in the Centennial State? How many UFO watchtowers? How many 42-foot hot dogs, taxis with disco balls, and monuments to headless chickens? How many cryogenically frozen Norwegian grandpas are there stashed away in Tuff Sheds? The answers to all these Colorado questions are the same: one. These unique attractions are what *Oddball Colorado* is all about.

Now let me ask you something else—and be honest—do your friends and coworkers really want to hear another story about that weekend you spent riding your mountain bike around in the hills? C'mon, *really*? What if, on the other hand, you regaled them with tales of an adventure through a vapor cave clad in little more than a towel, a pilgrimage to the state's best Rocky Mountain Oyster Bar, and a romantic evening at a drive-in movie . . . in a queen-size bed!?! These vacation opportunities are all in Colorado. You can visit odd museums dedicated to singular subjects such as buttons, keys, coins, bells, and brothels. You can find statues of cartoon characters, dead burros, and two-headed dragons. You can watch daring cliff divers as you chow down on Mexican food, or sit on the world's largest rocking chair, or bob along a lazy river past robotic mummies, but *only* if you will give those hiking boots a rest!

Don't get me wrong, I'm all for appreciating nature, breathing that fresh but thin mountain air, and getting a little exercise. But there has to be some balance. Somewhere in Oregon there's a large stump-covered hillside where all the trees used to create all the paper used to print the hundreds of Colorado travel guides on hiking trails, skiing getaways, and mountain biking were cut down. Do you want a two-sentence guide on finding an interesting place to hike? Get in your car, drive one hour in any direction, get out, and start walking. Colorado's gorgeous; you'll have fun. There it is—all the hiking advice you'll ever need, and I just saved a forest for you to walk through.

Now do yourself a favor: forget tackling Longs Peak, skiing the back bowls, or rafting down the Arkansas River this weekend. They'll still be there a month from now. Trust me. You've worked up enough sweat on your days off—why not take the time to laugh a little?

While I've tried to give clear directions from major streets and landmarks, you could still make a wrong turn. Bigfoot might be out there, so it's not time to panic. Remember these Oddball travel tips:

- **Stop and ask!** For a lot of communities, their Oddball attraction might be their only claim to fame. Locals are often thrilled that you'd drive out of your way to marvel at their underappreciated shrine. But choose your guides wisely: old cranks at the town cafe are good for information; pimply teenage clerks at the 7-Eleven are not.

- **Call ahead.** Few Oddball sites keep regular hours, but most will gladly wait around if they know you're coming. Some Colorado sites are seasonal; consequently, they can be closed for the winter at a moment's notice, particularly if there's an avalanche. Always call.

- **Don't give up.** Think of the woman who's sitting in a tiny museum dedicated to an obscure topic. She passed up a buyout offer from Starbucks because she cares about what she's doing. She didn't give up, and neither should you.

- **Don't trespass!** Don't become a Terrible Tourist. Just because somebody built a sculpture garden in their front yard doesn't mean they're looking for visitors. Ask permission or stay on the road.

- **Respect Colorado laws.** No matter how frustrated you may become, watch your language around your picnic basket or cooler—it is illegal in this state to insult fruits, vegetables, or dairy products.

Do you have an Oddball site of your own? Have I missed anything? Do you know of an Oddball site that should be included in a later version? Please write and let me know: Chicago Review Press, 814 North Franklin Street, Chicago, Illinois 60610.

ODDBALL COLORADO

DENVER AREA

What do you think of when you think of Denver? The Broncos? Skiing? The Orange Crush? The mountains? John Elway? Geez, you gotta break up the routine.

How about Mexican cliff divers? Art deco amusement parks? Robotic mummies? Defiled graveyards? Button museums? Tiny towns with tiny railroads? Yep, they're all here, too, though they're not often front-and-center in most travel publications . . . and isn't that a shame?

This chapter's collection of local sites delves into the weirder side of the Queen City of the Plains. Where did Buffalo Bill draw his last breath? Where did the cheeseburger draw its first breath? Where is there a religious shrine where it's difficult to draw *any* breath? While in search of answers to these questions, you'll have your tie cut off by a cowbell-clanging waitress, hear the true story behind the Old West's cowboys, and find out how many government workers it takes to change a lightbulb.

Denver
B-1 Bomber

From the beginning, the B-1 bomber was a political hot potato. This super-sonic, super-expensive bomber was killed by President Carter in 1977 as too costly for the nation's strategic defense, not to mention unnecessary. Ronald Reagan disagreed, and it was one of the many issues he used to defeat Carter in 1980.

Only four B-1s had been built before the plug was pulled. Those craft were dubbed B-1As when Reagan resurrected development on what became known as the B-1B. The second of the original B-1A prototypes is part of the Wings Over the Rockies collection.

It's a spooky, awkward-looking plane. The fuselage looks too fat for its narrow wings; its entire nose section, the Crew Escape Capsule, was designed to separate in an emergency to avoid having pilots eject at speeds over Mach 1. Go ahead, take a good look—you paid $325 million for each plane!

The museum has dozens of other aircraft, including a B-52 Strato-fortress, an H-21C "Flying Banana" helicopter, a German Luftwaffe trainer, and a *Star Wars* X-Wing Fighter. (No, Luke, you cannot take that last one out on a mission to blow up the Death Star.) If you're into space, local corporation Lockheed-Martin has donated an unused module intended for the International Space Station. And surrounding the central hangar are smaller spaces with aircraft-themed exhibits, such as WWI and WWII memorabilia, and the meeting room from Ike's Denver White House, moved from Lowry's Building 256, Room 230.

Wings Over the Rockies Air and Space Museum, The Hangar, 7711 E. Academy Blvd., Denver, CO 80230

(303) 360-5360

Hours: Monday–Saturday 10 A.M.–5 P.M., Sunday Noon–5 P.M.

Cost: Adults $4, Seniors (60+) $2, Kids (6–17) $2

www.wingsovertherockies.org

Directions: Three blocks east of Quebec St. at 1st Ave.

DENVER

Singer **Judy Collins** graduated from Denver's East High School in 1957.

Behold, the Messiah!

It's not every day the Messiah comes through town, yet Francis Schlatter came through Denver *twice*. The first time was in 1891, and few people took notice. This French cobbler had a shoe shop downtown on Stout Street. When he wasn't repairing shoes, he stared straight ahead like a zombie and rambled on about "The Master" who would soon bestow upon him healing powers. After a friend marveled that

You again?!!??

Photo courtesy of the Denver Public Library, F-7591

Schlatter had healed him, others dropped by for cures. Yet before he could develop his healing practice, he disappeared in July 1893.

Shoe Repair Shop, 1845 Stout St., Denver, CO 80202

No phone

Hours: Torn down

Cost: Free

Directions: Between 18th and 19th Sts., where the federal courthouse stands today.

Where did Schlatter go? Some say he wandered through the Mojave Desert, fasting, charming wild rattlesnakes, and healing the poor. He reappeared in New Mexico in July 1895, and he had a new message: he was the reincarnated spirit of Jesus. Denver alderman/businessman Edward Fox liked the sound of *that* and arranged to bring Schlatter back to town. Schlatter soon moved into Fox's home at 33rd Avenue and Quivas Street.

Word got around and hundreds were flocking to the Mile High City for cures. Fox built a stage in his front yard for folks to receive the Messiah's blessings. If Schlatter couldn't lay his hands on the faithful, he laid his hands on handkerchiefs that were mailed out. More than 60,000 people visited him over a two-month period.

Mimicking the story of Jesus, Schlatter claimed he would be called home by "The Father," and he had the date: November 16, 1895. The push was on for last-minute healings, but the self-proclaimed Messiah skipped town four days early. The disappointed mob outside Fox's house tore down the platform and fences—apparently they were well enough to riot.

Miners found Schlatter's bones in the mountains of New Mexico in 1897.

Schlatter Home, W. 33rd Ave. & Quivas St., Denver, CO 80211
No phone
Hours: Torn down
Cost: Free
Directions: On the southwest corner of 33rd Ave. and Quivas St., two blocks north of I-25.

Black American West Museum & Heritage Center

Think of the pop culture icons of the American cowboy in the Old West—John Wayne, Roy Rogers, Dale Evans, the Lone Ranger—and what did they share in common? Well, for one, they were all white. Heck, even their *horses* were white. And if you're thinking, "So? What's your point?" perhaps you should stop by this small museum with a big mission: to "Tell It Like It Was."

And how was it? Not even founder Paul Stewart knew at first. He'd grown up with the same lily-white image of the cowboys. As an African American child, he'd often wondered if there were any black cowboys. As an adult he investigated, and found out there were a lot of black cowboys. In fact, one out of every three cowboys was black, many of them ex-slaves who'd left the South for freer, greener pastures out west.

Stewart's collection of artifacts, historic research, and personal histories became the seed for this unique museum that touches not only on the lives of cowboys like Bill Pickett, "The Father of Bulldogging," but other black pioneers in the region. The museum is located in the restored (and relocated) former home of Justina Ford, M.D., Denver's

first black female doctor. Between 1902 and 1952, Ford delivered more than 7,000 babies, most of them in private homes because black people could not be admitted to city hospitals.

3901 California St., Denver, CO 80205

(303) 292-2566

E-mail: bawhc@aol.com

Hours: May–September, Daily 10 A.M.–5 P.M.; October–April, Wednesday–Friday 10 A.M.–2 P.M., Saturday–Sunday 10 A.M.–5 P.M.

Cost: Adults $6, Seniors (65+) $5.50, Kids (5–12) $4

www.coax.net/people/lwf/bawmus.htm

Directions: Just west of Downing at 30th St.

We'd like a Great Dane bag for our four-pound steak . . .
Photo courtesy of the Buckhorn Exchange

Buckhorn Exchange

Have you ever wondered what a saloon in the Old West was *really* like? Then mosey on over to the Buckhorn Exchange, Denver's first official restaurant/drinking establishment. Don't believe it? Check out the liquor license over the bar: Number 1.

The Buckhorn was started in 1893 by Henry "Shorty Scout" Zietz, a scout and friend of many Western figures, including Teddy Roosevelt, Sitting Bull, and Buffalo Bill. It has been a favorite of celebrities ever since, including James Cagney, Jimmy Carter, J. Edgar Hoover, Dwight Eisenhower, Bob Hope, Ronald Reagan, Will Rogers, Charlton Heston, and Roy Rogers, just to name a few.

Five hundred mounted animals cover the walls, many bagged over the years by the Zietz family. Not all are in traditional poses; they've got an antelope cut lengthwise, the back end of a deer, a two-headed calf, and a beefalo. Don't miss the jackalope and the "duffle bird," a rare fowl that eats hot chili peppers and flies backward to cool its tail feathers.

Dozens of other critters grace the menu. You can chow down on buffalo, alligator, rabbit, elk, rattlesnake, moose, and of course, beef. They're prepared the way they were a century ago, with ingredients like juniper berries, spring onions, and dried fruit. The priciest item on the menu is a four-pound $160 steak that feeds five.

The Buckhorn Exchange has always remained true to its heritage. The building is on the National Historic Register, and the mural on its north face was painted by Native Americans years ago. Each February the restaurant hosts a Buffalo Bill Look-Alike Contest.

1000 Osage St., Denver, CO 80204

(303) 534-9505

E-mail: info@buckhorn.com

Lunch Hours: Monday–Friday 11 A.M.–2 P.M.

Dinner Hours: Monday–Thursday 5:30–9 P.M., Friday–Saturday 5–10 P.M., Sunday 5–9 P.M.

Cost: Lunches $8–$11; Dinners $19–$39

www.buckhorn.com

Directions: Five blocks west of Santa Fe Dr. at 10th St.

DENVER

Actor **Peter Fonda** was detained at Denver's old Stapleton International Airport for disturbing the peace in July 1984. He had torn up the poster of a Lyndon LaRouche supporter that read, "Feed Jane Fonda to the Whales."

Buffalo Bill Death Site

Everyone's got to go sometime—even the roughest, toughest cowboy in the west. Buffalo Bill Cody was broke when he and his wife ended up at the home of his sister, May Cody Decker. When the end drew near, Cody was baptized as a Catholic at the request of his wife. He died a day later on January 10, 1917.

Though penniless, Cody's funeral was anything but spartan, thanks to his old friends. In fact, the ceremony was declared to be "Denver's gaudiest" by a local paper. That would have pleased the former showman. Cody was laid out in a glass-topped coffin on a purple couch at the Colorado Capitol building where a master of ceremonies hustled along 25,000 viewers who had come to pay their respects. Those who missed the event could see his casket while it was later paraded down 16th Street from the capitol to the Elks Hall.

Cody's widow claimed her husband wanted to be laid to rest atop Lookout Mountain, and locals were happy to oblige (see page 28).

2932 Lafayette St., Denver, CO 80205

Private phone

Hours: Always visible; view from street

Cost: Free

Directions: Two blocks east of Downing St., between 29th and 30th Sts.

Cheesman Park: Defiled Graveyard

Unsettling though it may be, when you stroll through Denver's Cheesman Park, you're treading on the defiled dead. The park and the adjacent Denver Botanic Gardens stand on what was once City Cemetery. Started in 1858 by then-mayor William Larimer, it was designed in such a way that high-class people were planted at the top of the hill, and lowlifes at the bottom.

Though the cemetery was still being filled, prairie dogs and grazing cattle began to take over. Word around town was that this was no longer the fashionable place to be buried, and people began shopping around. The land fell further into disrepair when the Catholic and Jewish communities moved their bodies elsewhere. But the secular city-managed plots remained until City Hall ordered all graves moved in 1893 to make room for development. Living Denver residents were told to move their dead relatives within 90 days or the bodies would be turned over to contractors to exhume.

The scene was ghastly. Workers were paid $1.90 for each corpse they dug up and transported to Riverside Cemetery (see page 21). To save money and space, the city asked contractors to place the exhumed into smaller coffins. Try to shoehorn a 6-foot corpse into a 1-by-3½-foot coffin and you'll begin to appreciate the depth of the problem.

Workers began unearthing coffins, prying them open, and rehousing the dead. Corpses were stripped of their valuables, broken into pieces or folded in half, and thrown into whichever boxes were available. Bones and body parts were left lying around on the ground. Neighbors were understandably upset, and the Denver papers shamed Mayor Platt Rogers into halting the project. That only made the problem worse. The site was abandoned for almost 10 years before the remaining bones were plowed under for the new park.

Today, psychics claim that disturbed souls still haunt the park and the homes adjoining the grounds. Neighbors sometimes see gunslinging pioneer ghosts in their mirrors. Given the events that happened here, is it any wonder?

13th Ave. & Franklin St., Denver, CO 80203

No phone

Hours: Always visible

Cost: Free

Directions: Thirteen blocks east of the State Capitol; bounded by 8th Ave., Franklin St., 13th Ave., and Race St.

Denver Mint

There are only two mints currently in operation in the United States. The largest, moved to this building in 1904, is where more than 12 billion coins are pressed each year. That's 48 million coins *each day*. The entire process is open to public viewing from an observation walkway. At the end of the line, workers bag up coins in thick canvas bags that are much too heavy to walk off with . . . so don't even think about it.

Gold ingots, on the other hand, are slightly more manageable. Just ask Orville Harrington. This night-shift worker hobbled out the front door with 53 gold ingots, one at a time, hidden in his hollowed-out wooden leg. The Secret Service caught up with him in 1920 and recovered the gold (valued at $80,000) buried in his yard at 1485 S. University Boulevard.

A more successful robbery took place here on December 18, 1922, though the mint is quick to point out that it didn't happen *inside*. Gunmen met a Federal Reserve Bank armored car as it pulled up on Colfax Avenue and, after a gun battle, walked away with $200,000 in five-dollar bills. One guard and one thief died in the shoot-out.

The Denver Mint is also one of three gold depositories in the United States. Fort Knox and West Point are the others. Approximately 25 percent of our nation's reserves lie a few floors beneath your feet on the tour. You were once able to see a few gold bars on the tour, stacked up like firewood in a vault. But ever since the Oklahoma City bombing, the door has been closed tight.

320 W. Colfax Ave., Denver, CO 80204

(303) 405-4761 or (303) 405-4765

Hours: Monday–Friday 8 A.M.–3 P.M.

Cost: Free

www.usmint.gov

Directions: Four blocks west of the State Capitol at Cherokee St.

DENVER

"[Denver] is probably the most self-sufficient, isolated, self-contained, and complacent city in the world."   —John Gunther

---

"I apprehend that there have been, during my two weeks sojourn [in Denver], more brawls, more fights, more pistol shots with criminal intent in this log city of one hundred and fifty dwellings, not three-fourths completed, nor two-thirds inhabited, nor one-third fit to be, than in any community of no greater numbers on earth."   —Horace Greeley

---

"The air [in Denver] is so refined that you can live without much lungs."   —Shane Leslie

THE CHEESEBURGER
Humpty Dumpty Drive-In, 2776 Speer Blvd.

Burned down. Louis Ballast had the good fortune to be clumsy—he spilled cheddar cheese onto his hamburger grill during the early 1930s, and the cheeseburger was born! His barrel-shaped Humpty Dumpty Drive-In became a must-stop eatery, even during the Depression. Ballast received a patent for the name *Cheese Burger* in 1935, though he no longer has exclusive rights.

THE DENVER BOOT
Marugg Pattern Works, 1218 Wazee St.

Torn down. It started as a nice idea: a simple locking device was sold to car owners to prevent thieves from snagging tires in rubber-hungry WWII America. Metal worker Frank Marugg built the first Denver Boot in 1944, but it was mostly forgotten after Hitler was defeated. One person who didn't forget, however, was Dan Stills, head of the city's traffic division in the early 1950s. His department had come under criticism for auto break-ins at the car pound. So Stills asked Marugg to make an improved Denver Boot that officers could use to immobilize violators' cars where they parked. The first unlucky resident was cuffed in January 1955, and the city has been at it ever since.

THE VFW POST
John S. Stewart VFW Post #1, 955 Bannock St., (303) 571-5659

The nation's first Veterans of Foreign Wars Post, John S. Stewart Post #1, still stands south of downtown, established in 1901. Stop on by for a visit, and ask the bartender to see if one of the vets can take you on a tour of the museum in the meeting room. The hall has glass cases filled with military equipment and souvenirs from every conflict since the Civil War, all of which were fought on foreign soil.

THE ICE CREAM SODA
Baur's Restaurant During the summer of 1871, a customer entered Otto P. Baur's restaurant and asked for a *reeeeally* cold soda. Unfortunately, Baur had run out of ice. No problem, he substituted ice cream, and the ice cream soda was born.

DENVER: MILE HIGH BIRTHPLACE

SHREDDED WHEAT

Henry Perky's Home Shredded Wheat was invented in Denver in 1893 at the home of Henry Perky. This health fanatic originally made it for his own consumption. The process involved boiling, extruding, and drying raw wheat, then baking it. Soon others were buying it in quantities so large that he needed an industrial facility. Perky couldn't find a suitable location in Denver, but Niagara Falls, New York, coaxed him into establishing the operation at a waterfall-powered plant in 1900.

DIAGONAL CROSSWALKS

All over the City Denver traffic engineering guru Henry Barnes invented the nation's first "all stop" lights in Denver during the 1930s. With all cars at a complete halt, pedestrians could walk diagonally across intersections. Some dubbed these arrangements Barnes Dances. Barnes was also a pioneer in synchronized traffic lights.

DENVER

When the Detroit Pistons beat the Denver Nuggets 186–183 in 1983, it was the highest total scoring basketball game ever.

Fleeing her parents' plan for an arranged marriage in Milwaukee, the future Israeli prime minister **Golda Meir** arrived at the home of her sister Shayna Korngold in Denver (1606–08 Julian St.). Here she met her future husband. The home was moved to Habitat Park (1156 Ninth St.) in 1982, where you can find it today.

Rick James suffered a neck aneurysm at the Mammoth Events Center (now the Fillmore Auditorium, Colfax Ave. & Clarkson St.) on November 6, 1998, after too many super-freaky tosses of his head. Doctors diagnosed him with "rock 'n' roll neck." The aneurysm caused a blood clot that went to his brain, causing a stroke a week later.

Denver Museum of Miniatures, Dolls, and Toys

Just west of City Park is a unique Victorian home filled with many more Victorian homes . . . and adobe pueblos . . . and Newport mansions.

Welcome to the Denver Museum of Miniatures, Dolls, and Toys! Every room in this enormous home is crammed with old doll houses, Kachina dolls, tin toys, and teeny-weeny furniture. While many have been acquired, others were made by museum members specifically for display here. One of the strangest collections is a room with tiny haunted houses— see a front porch decked out for trick-or-treaters, take a peek into Vincent Price's attic, or see what a witch has stashed away in her closets.

In addition to the toys on display, the museum has plenty of toys out for children to play with. These goodies come in handy; kids aren't tortured by seeing toys they can't play with, and adults aren't distracted by bored kids.

1880 N. Gaylord St., Denver, CO 80206

(303) 322-1053

E-mail: Idsbc@aol.com

Hours: Tuesday–Saturday, 10 A.M.–4 P.M., Sunday 1–4 P.M.

Cost: Adults $5, Seniors (62+) $4, Kids (2–16) $4

www.dmmdt.homepage.com

Directions: One block west of York St., north of 18th St.

DENVER LAWS

➡ Before a dog catcher goes after a pooch, he or she must warn that dog with a posted notice.

➡ You may not lead a cattle drive through the streets of Denver.

➡ Horseback riders may not exceed 20 MPH.

➡ Mistreating rats is illegal in the Mile High City.

➡ It is against the law to wear a false face.

➡ Dogs in Denver must pay full fare on trams, and cannot purchase transfers.

➡ Smelly people cannot ride streetcars.

➡ Borrowing your neighbor's vacuum cleaner is illegal in Denver.

Forney Museum of Transportation

The Forney Museum of Transportation has long been Denver's best museum of buggies, trains, and automobiles. It recently moved from an abandoned and dusty warehouse along I-25 to a larger space next to the National Western Stock Show. Now everything is indoors—even the trains. Classic auto lovers will get the most out of this collection that includes:

- Amelia Earhart's yellow "Goldbug" Kissel
- Nepalese Prince Aly Kahn's 1927 New Phantom Rolls-Royce with its gold-plated hood and wheels
- Admiral Richard Byrd's 1915 Cadillac
- German Ambassador General Von Wagner's wheelchair-accessible 1928 Mercedes-Benz; it was confiscated by the United States at the onset of World War II
- A 1975 Pontiac "Zabeast" art car covered in bumper stickers
- Messerschmitt's 1955 three-wheeled Cabin Scooter KR-20, made with a leftover airplane engine from World War II
- An energy-saving 1981 Freeway built by H-M-V Vehicles, designed to triple gas mileage on long hauls

A funky addition to the new Forney Museum is a collection of famous figures bought at auction from a defunct wax museum. No longer do you have to imagine Amelia in her "Goldbug"—she's sitting in it! For some reason, W. C. Fields is standing off by himself, and the Wright Brothers are planeless. Former Colorado Governor William Gilpin hangs around in the snack lounge to make sure you've cleaned up after yourself.

4303 Brighton Blvd., Denver, CO 80216

(303) 297-1113

E-mail: forney@frii.net

Hours: Monday–Saturday 9 A.M.–5 P.M.

Cost: Adults $6, Seniors $5, Teens (12–18) $4, Kids (5–11) $2

www.forneymuseum.com

Directions: Just south of I-70 from the Brighton Blvd. exit.

If You Like Ike . . .

Though he was born in Texas and raised in Kansas, Dwight D. Eisenhower was as attached to Colorado as anywhere in the country. As a military man, he spent time on army bases throughout the world, but his wife, Mamie,

had Denver roots. She was born in Iowa, but Mamie Doud graduated from Denver's Wolcott School for Girls in 1914. Two years later, on July 11, 1916, she married Dwight in a simple ceremony at her mother Elivera's house in the Capitol Hill neighborhood. They honeymooned near Boulder in Eldorado Springs.

Ike & Mamie Marriage Site, 750 Lafayette St., Denver, CO 80218
Private phone
Hours: Private residence; view from street
Cost: Free
Directions: One block north of 6th Ave., two blocks east of Downing.

Dwight and Mamie Eisenhower lived all over the nation following World War I but ended up living back at Elivera's place on the eve of World War II. Imagine, in a few short years he went from freeloading son-in-law to Supreme Allied Commander. After the war, the couple returned here for a short while.

When it came time to run for president in 1952, Ike used a suite at the Brown Palace as his national campaign headquarters. If you plop down $925 for the Eisenhower Suite, you can be sure you're staying in Ike's former digs by checking out the divot in the fireplace molding. Ike supposedly made that when he sliced an in-room golf shot.

Brown Palace, 321 Seventeenth St., Denver, CO 80202
(800) 321-2599 or (303) 297-3111
Hours: Always open
Cost: Free; Rooms $125–$375/night; Suites $350–$925/night
www.brownpalace.com
Directions: Corner of 17th St. and Broadway.

As the housekeeping staff at the Brown Palace learned, Ike loved golf. Even with the weight of the Free World on his shoulders, he always found time for a few rounds. Near the end of his summer-long Denver vacation in 1955 (see Wings Over the Rockies, page 2), he played 27 holes at a local course. The next day, he was admitted to Fitzsimmons Army Hospital where he suffered a massive heart attack on September 24, 1955. Rather than let the American public worry, his handlers downplayed the severity of his medical condition. Ike was not released from the hospital until November 11.

Fitzsimmons Army Hospital, Ursula St. & 17th Pl., Aurora, CO 80045

No phone

Hours: Always visible

Cost: Free

Directions: Two blocks north of Colfax Ave., two blocks east of Peoria St.

JHB Button Museum

They hold up your pants, hold down your collar, and keep your shirt or blouse together—buttons! Most folks lose more of these things than they find, but not Jean Barr, founder of JHB International. Her company is not a manufacturer but a distributor. If there is a button to be had, chances are it'll find its way to the offices of JHB. A sample of each and every one is on display at the Button Museum: round, square, fish-shaped, flower-shaped, shell-shaped, two-holed, four-holed, plastic, metal, bone, cloth-covered, cheap, expensive . . . and in every color under the sun. They've got everything but belly buttons, and your tour guide has one of those.

The museum also has a large collection of thimbles, which come in handy if you're sewing on buttons. You'll also get to see the process by which buttons imported in bulk are attached to little cards for retail sale. Fascinating!

JHB International, Inc., 1955 S. Quince St., Denver, CO 80231

(303) 751-8100

Hours: Monday–Friday 2:30–4:30 P.M., by appointment only

Cost: Free

www.buttons.com

Directions: Two blocks north of Evans Ave. on Quebec St., then east on Jewell Ave. to Quince St.

Lakeside Amusement Park

Forget that unnamed, overrated amusement park near downtown! Denver's *best* amusement park is century-old Lakeside. Hugging the shores of Lake Rhonda, Lakeside is a throwback to the 1920s with its art deco styling. It is best appreciated after dark when it is illuminated by miles of neon and billions of tiny lightbulbs.

The park was founded in 1908, and one of its first rides was the two coal-burning trains from the 1904 St. Louis World's Fair that circled the lake.

The wooden Cyclone roller coaster long held the record for the highest speed at the bottom of the first hill, and still makes the nation's Top 10 favorites of coaster enthusiasts. If you're on a budget, and don't mind crowds, come on July 4 for Dime Day, or check out Nickel Days on Labor Day weekend.

4601 Sheridan Blvd., Denver, CO 80212

(303) 477-1621

E-mail: information@lakesideamusementpark.com

Hours: May, Saturday–Sunday Noon–11 P.M.; June–August, Monday–Friday 6–11 P.M., Saturday–Sunday Noon–11 P.M.

Cost: Monday–Friday, Adults $11.25 (all day pass)+ $1.50 (gate admission); Saturday–Sunday, Adults $14.75 (all day pass)+ $1.50 (gate admission)

www.lakesideamusementpark.com

Directions: Two blocks south of the Sheridan Blvd. exit from I-70.

Gettin' high!

Mile High Step

Denver is known as the Mile High City, and the thirteenth step of the State Capitol is the reason. Carved into the front of the step is the proclamation, "One Mile Above Sea Level." There's only one problem with this statement: it's wrong. A survey in 1969 determined that the step was actually 5,279 feet high, so a new marker was embedded just above the fifteenth step.

Whew—it's a good thing they got that settled!

Considering when it was built, it was lucky the capitol's elevation was even close to being correct. Builders broke ground in 1886, but it wasn't until 1908 that the structure was finished. The dome was originally coated with copper, but state boosters objected and it was regilded with 200 ounces of gold. After catching a few folks at the downspouts over the years, the state legislature passed a law making it illegal to pan for gold in the roof's runoff.

Colorado State Capitol, 200 E. Colfax Ave., Denver, CO 80203

(303) 866-2604

Tour Hours: September–May, Monday–Friday 9:30 A.M.–3:30 P.M.; June–August,
  Monday–Saturday 9:30 A.M.–2:30 P.M.

Cost: Free

www.archives.state.co.us/cap/first.htm

Directions: At the corner of Broadway and Colfax Ave. (15th Ave.).

EVERYONE'S A MILE HIGH . . .

Take a quick look through the Denver phone book and you'll find that businesses all over the city are a mile high:

- Mile High Reptiles
- Mile High Foot Clinic
- Mile High Embroidery
- Mile High Calcium
- Mile High Nannies
- Mile-High Babes
- Mile High Pianos
- Mile High Pipes & Tobacco
- Mile High Dream Institute
- Mile High Cheerleading Training Center
- Mile Hi Elevator Inspection
- Mile High Roll-Off Waste Systems
- Mile Hi Nails
- Mile Hi-Draulics, Inc.
- Mile High Tattoo
- Mile Hi Statuary
- Mile High Crankshafts
- Mile High Chimney Sweep
- Mile High Basements

The Murder of Alan Berg

When radio talk show host Alan Berg was gunned down outside his Denver apartment on June 18, 1984, a lot of jerks thought he had been "asking for it." Berg was known for his confrontational style, baiting the likes of the Ku Klux Klan, jingoistic politicians, conservative pundits, pointy-headed liberals, and any other loud-mouth, hypocritical bonehead he encountered, not to mention a few well-intentioned but naïve callers. Using his experience as a former trial lawyer, Berg would carve up his guests and listeners with equal enthusiasm and delight.

But it would be wrong to say that Berg was mean. He was certainly blunt, often outrageous, and he would hang up on callers if he thought they were morons (and usually told them so before he did). But he also provided otherwise conservative Colorado with an unflinching, undogmatic liberal point of view. And he was popular, even with those who admitted he was "the guy you loved to hate."

That didn't sit well with the likes of The Order, a Fascist organization from the Pacific Northwest. This nasty collection of neo-Nazis gunned down Berg as he got out of his Volkswagen in front of his apartment—shot him in the back as he was coming home to feed his dog. That was brave. It took years before the FBI discovered who had killed Berg, getting their break only after members of The Order had killed several federal agents. (The Berg murder was later fictionalized in Eric Bogosian's *Talk Radio*.)

Berg's killing turned out to be an ominous first volley from a growing movement of heavily armed, right-wing extremists bent on destroying the federal government: Aryan Nations, Posse Comitatus, and free floaters like Timothy McVeigh. Too bad so few people paid attention.

1445 Adams St., Denver, CO 80206

Private phone

Hours: Always visible; view from street

Cost: Free

Directions: Just south of Colfax Ave. (15th Ave.), seven blocks west of Colorado Blvd., in front of garage door on the left.

DENVER
Denver's Colfax Avenue is the longest continuous street in the United States.

Thanks for nothin', Neil!

Neil Bush, Numskull

You hear a lot about George Bush's sons George W. and Jeb, but who remembers Neil? Well, a whole lot of folks who had accounts with Denver's Silverado Savings and Loan, that's who. Though he had no banking experience, Neil Bush was given a job on this Denver S&L's 11-seat board of directors in 1985. He soon was signing off on pay raises for the later-indicted heads at the institution, and faulty accounting reports from later-fined auditor Coopers and Lybrand. (Can anyone say "mini-Enron"?) Silverado was staying solvent mainly through rampant speculation in risky commercial real estate ventures made possible by Reagan-era deregulation. Meanwhile, it was offering higher interest rates to its depositors than it was demanding on its loans, and it doesn't take a math genius to realize that's a formula that can't work forever.

Depending on who you asked, Bush's family connections appeared to pay off in 1988 when his vice-president father was running for president. Keeping things quiet, the collapsing Silverado was propped up by a $450 million loan from the federal Home Loan Bank in August 1988; even that didn't help much. By October, auditors recommended the FDIC take over, but internally the feds ordered a delay until November 9, as in the day after November 8, the day after George Bush's election victory.

In all, taxpayers were out $1 billion for Silverado, which sounds like a lot, but it was a mere fraction of the $450 billion in S&L collapses nationwide in the same scandal. Taxpayers and depositors paid the eventual price. The FDIC sued the former directors, accounting firms, and legal counsel for Silverado for $49.5 million, and were paid in part from a $23 million defense fund set up by the directors for just this eventuality—using Silverado cash, of course. That's planning! Neil Bush ended up paying $50,000 out of his own pocket and—this is the best part—was banned by the Office of Thrift Supervision from ever getting involved in banking *for the rest of his life*. Thank heaven for small favors—them Bush young 'uns ain't good with numberals.

Silverado (former headquarters), 3900 Mexico Ave., Denver, CO 80210

No phone

Hours: Always visible

Cost: Free

Directions: Two blocks north of I-25 on Colorado Blvd.

DENVER

If you like gargoyles, stop by the home at 2145 N. York Street in Denver. In addition to dozens of winged statues, the front yard has a carved tree called "The Enchanted Forest" by David Leon Mitchell.

. . . thank ya ver-uh much!

Riverside Cemetery

Riverside Cemetery may not be in the best part of town, wedged as it is between industrial lots, the South Platte floodplain, and Commerce City's western boundary, but it boasts some of this state's most famous residents and most interesting monuments.

The names on the tombstones are a virtual Who's Who of Colorado pioneers, from former territorial and state governors, Denver mayors, influential settlers, and a few strange surprises. (You should purchase a guidebook at the cemetery office to fully appreciate them all.) Riverside has the graves of Augusta Tabor, spurned wife of Horace; Clara Brown and Barney Ford, both influential African American pioneers featured in the stained glass windows of the State Capitol; governors John Routt, John Evans, and John Elbert; and Jeremiah and Emily Lee, successful miner and nurse respectively, he a former slave of Robert E. Lee and she a descendant of one of George Washington's slaves.

Riverside is also known for several remarkable monuments, including a replica of Lester Drake's cabin, right down to a pile of stone animal poop out back; a bareback Arabian stallion named Ali atop Addison Baker's plot, the only such horse in any American cemetery; and the Frank

Shy Memorial, a carved pet dog guarding the 13-year-old's remains. But perhaps the best monuments in the entire boneyard are those of Rudolph Pigeon and William Larson. Pigeon was the real name of Shorty Maynard, a circus clown who is remembered for his trained geese and bucking mule— Shorty's face is on the headstone (Block 13). The marker over Larson's grave (Block 16) does not show the man laid out beneath it, but Elvis Presley in a Vegas jumpsuit. Now *that's* a fan!

Riverside Cemetery, 5201 Brighton Blvd., Denver, CO 80216

(303) 293-2466

Hours: Daily 9 A.M.–5 P.M.

Cost: Free

Directions: On the north side of Brighton Blvd. (Rte. 265), just west of York St. on the Denver–Commerce City border.

Roseanne's Big Break

In 1971, Roseanne (Barr, at the time) arrived in Colorado with one goal in mind: to get the hell out of Utah. After that, she didn't have much of a plan. She was 19 at the time and had told her parents she was going to live with her sister in Denver. She landed just short, in Georgetown. There she fell quickly into love and codependency with the night clerk at the Georgetown Motor Inn (1100 Rose St., (303) 569–3201), Bill Pentland. He had wowed her on their first date by serving her leftover Hamburger Helper, playing Joni Mitchell records, and washing her hair.

In the fall of 1972, the two moved into a trailer parked across the street from a Georgetown cemetery. A year and a half later, while on acid and watching a horror film on television, they grew paranoid about their living arrangement. They raced off to a justice of the peace in Golden and were married on February 4, 1974. From there, they spent a brief time in a Manitou Springs trailer park where their first child was born, then landed in Denver (3130 S. Utica) in 1976, where they had another child.

Roseanne spent the next several years raising the kids and battling anorexia (true!) and the isolation of being at home. Finally, she took a job at Bennigan's (2550 Canyon Blvd., Boulder) where she developed a cult following of customers who were charmed by her in-your-face rudeness. With her sister's help, she began developing her act in Denver's underground entertainment world: punk bars, biker hangouts, lesbian coffee shops, and feminist bookstores. She generated enough attention to get a few nights at clubs like the Comedy Shoppe and the Comedy Store. In 1980 she won the annual Denver Laugh-Off at the Comedy Works beating out a field of 15 men. She lost no time in heading for Los Angeles, and was on the *Tonight Show* within a month.

Comedy Works, 1226 15th St., Denver, CO 80202

(303) 595-3637

Hours: Always visible. Showtimes are Sunday and Tuesday–Thursday 8 P.M., Friday 8 and 10 P.M., Saturday 6:30, 8:30, and 10:30 P.M.

Cost: Tickets vary

www.comedyworks.com

Directions: Downtown at 15th and Lawrence Sts.

Talking Sidewalk

If you find yourself walking downtown along Curtis Street, between 15th and 16th on the north side of the street, you're likely to hear the sound of a factory humming away beneath the grating, or a steam locomotive, or the chattering of monkeys in a rain forest.

No, you're not strolling along a haunted sidewalk; you're just walking all over somebody's art project. (Though it *could* be haunted; this is the former site of the Tabor Grand Opera House.) Ask around and nobody will fess up as to who put the speakers down there, why they did it, and why they're still running after all these years—but does it make a difference? The continuous loop of misplaced background noise amuses the locals and confuses the out-of-towners, which are two good reasons to keep it running.

1500–1600 Curtis St., Denver, CO 80202

No phone

Hours: Always there

Cost: Free

Directions: On Curtis St., between 15th and 16th Sts., on the north side of the street, adjacent to the Federal Reserve Branch Bank.

DENVER

Douglas Fairbanks was born in Denver on May 23, 1883, as Douglas Elton Thomas Ulman. He later attended West High School.

Nobody messes with mah trailers!

Trailer Park Cowboy

Life in a trailer park is no picnic. With wheels on their homes, your neighbors are often transient. Tornadoes seem to have it in for your type of lightweight dwelling. And then there are the constant, glaring lights from the *Cops* camera crews.

But the folks at the Rustic Ranch Mobile Home Park have none of those worries. With a 30-foot gun-packin' cowboy guarding the entrance, nobody would dare mess with these trailer folk. Rustic Ranch accents the western theme with log siding on the office, but that's about as far as it goes.

Rustic Ranch Mobile Home Park, 5565 Federal Blvd., Denver, CO 80221

(303) 477-0583

Hours: Always visible

Cost: Free

Directions: Two blocks north of I-76 on Federal Blvd.

Unsinkable Molly Brown House

Maggie Brown wanted desperately to be accepted by Denver's high society, but they would have none of it. To them she was nothing more than a Missouri hick who married into money when she snagged her husband James "J. J." Brown in Leadville. Some even dubbed her the American Warbler for her frequent yodeling.

But Maggie had the good fortune of being aboard the *Titanic* on its maiden voyage on the night of April 14, 1912. With characteristic feistiness, she rowed Lifeboat No. 6 to safety and was dubbed "The Unsinkable" Maggie Brown. Her then-separated spouse had another theory: "She's too mean to sink." (She was also too mean to kill; J.J. tried to shoot her twice without success.) The women of Denver's "Sacred 36" finally accepted her, if for no other reason than to hear her recount that perilous night in the North Atlantic. Over, and over, and over again.

The Browns' Denver home stands pretty much the way it did when the family lived there, thanks to Maggie's habit of photographing the interior rooms every time she changed the gaudy décor, which was often. She even changed the books in the library at Christmastime, checking out hundreds of red-and-green-spined titles from the local library to match the season. The front entryway's Turkish Corner closely resembles Graceland's cloth-draped Pool Room. The house is still flanked by the four lion statues, earning it the nickname The House of Lions.

Maggie Brown might have been forgotten to history were it not for a hit musical by Meredith Willson in 1960. The name Maggie didn't sound quite right, so he changed it to Molly, and the name stuck. She was never called Molly in her lifetime.

Some believe the building is haunted by Maggie and J.J. to this day. Maggie's ghost is usually accompanied by the smell of rosewater; sometimes her rocker tips back and forth by itself. J.J.'s ghost reportedly reeks of cigar smoke and hangs out in a different part of the house.

1340 Pennsylvania St., Denver, CO 80203

(303) 832-4092

Hours: June–August, Monday–Saturday 9:30 A.M.–4 P.M., Sunday Noon–4 P.M.; September–May, Tuesday–Saturday 10 A.M.–4 P.M., Sunday Noon–4 P.M.

Cost: Adults $6.50, Seniors (65+) $4.50, Kids (6–12) $2.50

www.mollybrown.org

Directions: Three blocks east of the State Capitol, one block south of Colfax Ave. (15th Ave.).

Suburbs
Commerce City
Geronimo!

Geronimo was a brave dog. Adopted by the 507th Parachute Regiment out of Fort Benning, Georgia, during World War II, he was taught to parachute behind enemy lines and to sniff out explosives. Geronimo was a mutt, and though he looked like a German shepherd, his loyalty was always to the good ol' U. S. of A. He traveled the nation raising money for war bonds, and sold more than $1 million. President Roosevelt was so impressed that he promoted the dog to sergeant, and kept a plaster cast of Geronimo's paw print in the Oval Office. Not even Eisenhower got that!

Though willing to fight on the front lines, Geronimo never saw action against the Axis. Instead, he was honorably discharged when his handler, Ken Williams, broke his leg in a training jump. Williams and Geronimo came west, where Geronimo was run over by a car in 1947.

Denver Pet Cemetery, 5721 E. 72nd Ave., Commerce City, CO 80022

(303) 288-0177

Hours: Daily 9 A.M.–5 P.M.

Cost: Free

Directions: Three blocks west of Rte. 2 on 72nd St.; grave to the left of the main building.

Englewood and Westminster
Traildust Steak Houses

Denver doesn't have many hoity-toity eateries with tie-and-jacket dress codes, yet there are two popular eateries on the other end of the spectrum where they'll cut off your tie if you dare to wear one: the Traildust Steak Houses. These restaurants give fair warning on their front doors—"No Neckties Beyond This Point!"—but still, people try to sneak by (mostly kids in their fathers' hideous leftovers). If you dare to dress up, your friendly server will turn into a scissors-wielding maniac, clanging a cowbell while sirens blare, until that white-collar noose is sliced from your neck. For your embarrassment, you're given a free drink and your tie is stapled to the wall with a million others that earlier met a similar fate.

Meat is the main menu offering at the Traildusts, from reasonably sized cuts to the 50-ounce, two-inch-thick Bull Shipper. Each restaurant has a slide from the second floor to the first, which lands patrons at the dance floor. The chutes are only closed when the live band is playing on Friday and Saturday nights, just to keep folks from slamming into the line dancers.

7101 S. Clinton, Englewood, CO 80112

(303) 790-2420

Hours: Monday–Thursday 5–10 P.M., Friday 5 P.M.–Midnight, Saturday 4 P.M.–Midnight,
   Sunday Noon–10 P.M.

Cost: $12–$30

www.traildust.com

Directions: One block east of I-25 on Arapaho, turn south on Clinton.

9101 Benton St., Westminster, CO 80030

(303) 427-1446

Hours: Monday–Thursday 5–10 P.M., Friday 5 P.M.–Midnight, Saturday 4 P.M.–Midnight,
   Sunday Noon–10 P.M.

Cost: $12–$30

www.traildust.com

Directions: Exit the Boulder Turnpike (Rte. 36) at Sheridan Blvd. heading west; restaurant
   is on the east side of the Westminster Mall.

Federal Heights
Lost River of the Pharaohs

Egyptian tombs in Colorado? That's right, but the only way to see them is to travel back in time on an inner tube. Whaaaat??? You heard correctly: the Lost River of the Pharaohs is an aquatic attraction at Water World, the nation's largest water park. It's a spooky voyage through pyramids

filled with animatronic mummies—much scarier than the nonrobotic
real ones found in musty historic museums.

And do you want to go back further in time? Check out the Voyage
to the Center of the Earth where dinosaurs rule over a lava-oozing
world. Need something a little calmer? Head over to Wally World, the
FunH$_2$Ouse, or the Lazy River. Daredevils can try the Zoomerang, the
Bermuda Triangle, or the multistory Thrill Hill body slide. And before
you towel off and head home, be sure you've tried out the Space Bowl
where you can experience what it's like to be flushed down a funnel,
(kind of like being in a toilet).

Water World, 1800 W. 89th Ave., Federal Heights, CO 80260

(303) 427-SURF

Hours: June–August, daily 10 A.M.–6 P.M. (weather permitting)

Cost: Adults $24.95, Seniors (60+) Free, Kids (5–12) $20.95

www.waterworldcolorado.com

Directions: At 88th St. and Pecos St., just west of I-25.

Golden
Buffalo Bill Museum and Grave

Burying Buffalo Bill atop Lookout Mountain was no easy task. First, he
died in the middle of winter and the ground was frozen solid. He wasn't
laid to rest until June 3, 1917, after the thaw. Then there was the problem
with potential body snatchers. Cody had to be planted in a steel-lined
vault, embedded in granite, under seven tons of concrete poured over
steel rebar. There was well-founded concern that his body might be
nabbed by rival tourist interests in Wyoming and Nebraska. (Much later,
in 1948, the American Legion Post in Cody, Wyoming, offered $10,000
to anyone who could deliver the body of the town's namesake.) Cody's
sturdy vault posed a problem when his wife needed to be buried years
later. Caretakers had to break open the tomb with a jackhammer, then
drop her casket on top of his.

From the very beginning, Buffalo Bill's grave site has been a tourist
trap. Unofficial foster son Johnny Baker opened the Pahaska Tepee, a
combination gift shop, museum, and snack bar serving all interests
Codyan. Years later a more formal museum took on the responsibility
for documenting Buffalo Bill's life. Here you can see relics from his Wild

West show, including his ivory-handled Colt "peacemaker," Sitting Bull's .44 Winchester repeater, costumes, and show posters. Learn how he earned his nickname, shooting 4,280 buffalo over 18 months to feed railroad workers during the westward expansion. They've even got one of those unlucky critters stuffed and on display. If you're here the last weekend in July, join in the Buffalo Bill Days celebrations.

987.5 Lookout Mountain Rd., PO Box 950, Golden, CO 80401

(303) 526-0747 or (303) 526-0744

Hours: May–October, daily 9 A.M.–5 P.M.; November–April, Tuesday–Saturday
  9 A.M.–4 P.M.

Museum Cost: Adults $3, Seniors (65+) $2, Kids (6–15) $1

www.buffalobill.org

Directions: Exit 256 from I-70, follow the signs to Lookout Mountain.

Mine Eyes No Longer See the Glory . . .

Sometimes you have to watch who you listen to. Back in 1991, former Wendy's manager Theresa Lopez claimed that the Virgin Mary had appeared to her on October 13 and November 10 claiming "great favors shall be rained upon you on my feast day." She and 6,000 pilgrims flocked to

Stairway to heaven?

Mother Cabrini Shrine on December 8, 1991, looking for a miracle.

Instead, many got permanent visual damage. When the faithful looked directly at the sun, they claimed it was spinning and shooting off brilliant colors. A local ophthalmologist suggested the personal light shows were more likely the last, dying signals from their retinal cells exploding. And he was right.

Undaunted, Lopez continued to have visions and encouraged the as-yet-unblind to the mountain shrine on the second Sunday of each month. Sometimes she was assisted by a trance medium named Reverend Jack Spaulding.

The Mother Cabrini Shrine is worth a visit, even without Lopez, but if you have a heart condition or aren't used to high altitudes, you might want to forgo the trek up the stations of the cross, which are laid out along the 373 steps to the summit, aptly dubbed the Stairway to Heaven. Instead, view the statues from the parking lot and take a chug or two from the holy spring. Supposedly, water gushed from a rock when Mother Cabrini struck it with a cane during a visit years ago. The cane is on display in the gift shop.

Mother Cabrini came through Denver years ago, and she attempted to ride a burro to the top of this hill. The stubborn critter stopped half-way and made her walk up herself. At the summit, Cabrini arranged a pile of rocks into the shape of the Sacred Heart. You can still see the pile today, protected under Plexiglas. While you're there, look for another circle of rocks near the statue; that's where Lopez had her visions.

Mother Cabrini Shrine, 20189 Cabrini Blvd., Golden, CO 80401

(303) 526-0758

Hours: Daily 7 A.M.–5:30 P.M. (7:30 P.M. summers)

Cost: Free

www.den-cabrini-shrine.org

Directions: Take Exit 259 from I-70, head west on the north-side frontage road (Rte. 40), and follow the signs.

Rocky Flats

How many government workers does it take to change a lightbulb? As it turns out, there's an answer: 43. Of course, that's only if everyone follows the 33-step procedure detailed in a federal guidebook. If nobody loafs on the job, the task should take a mere 1,087.1 hours. As you might have guessed, this manual wasn't referring to just any lightbulb, but one in a radioactive containment area at the former Rocky Flats Nuclear Weapons Facility.

Thankfully, there isn't much need for that guidebook anymore, because Rocky Flats is being decommissioned . . . and not a moment too soon. The facility was plagued with problems. Fires in 1957, 1966, 1969, and 1990 released radioactive material into the atmosphere upwind of the Denver metropolitan area. A grand jury concluded that because Rockwell International, which managed the plant at the height of its problems, had been hired by the Department of Energy, its employees couldn't be prosecuted because of governmental sovereignty. The site is part of the Superfund cleanup program. Workers expect to be finished by 2006. They'd be finished sooner, but that place had a lot of lightbulbs.

Today, a museum on the grounds tells what's being done to correct the contamination. Believe it or not, the plant is listed on the National Register of Historic Places.

Rocky Flats Environmental Technology Site, Route 93, PO Box 464, Golden, CO 80402
(303) 966-8164
Hours: Monday–Friday 6 A.M.–4:30 P.M.
Cost: Free
Directions: East off Foothills Rd. (Rte. 93) north of Coal Creek Canyon Rd. (Rte. 72).

GOLDEN

Golden police chased a wild kangaroo near town on August 12, 1976, but did not catch it.

The ghost of a man struck by a train that once ran along Route 93 near Golden still haunts the road. He wears a derby and stinks of rotting flesh.

The National Guard Armory in Golden is the largest cobblestone building in the United States.

Lakewood
Casa Bonita

The outside of this restaurant is deceiving. A Spanish mission façade in a strip mall looks intriguing, but it really gives no hint as to the magical wonders that will greet you just inside the front door.

First off, you file along in a chow line; everyone must buy a dinner. Your order is radioed to the kitchen, and just like on *Star Trek*, your meal pops through a little window onto your tray. The fun is just beginning.

Ask your host or hostess for a seat by the waterfall—everyone else does—and you just might get lucky. Much of the three-story restaurant wraps around a central pool where cliff divers plunge from the rocks to the water below.

Go ahead, wolf down your food and start exploring. More guests are up walking around than are sitting and eating. Wind your way through claustrophobic Black Bart's Cave behind the Puppet Theater. Break into and out of the Mexican Jail with its rubber bars. Check out one of the evening's magic shows at the downstairs theater, or look for gold in the Lost Mine. And don't miss the hourly gunfights and gorilla hunts on the stage by the waterfall! It's all included as part of your evening at the best restaurant in town.

6715 W. Colfax Ave., Denver, CO 80214

(303) 232-5115

Hours: Sunday–Thursday 11 A.M.–9:30 P.M., Friday–Saturday 11 A.M.–10 P.M.

Cost: Meals $7–$12

www.casabonitadenver.com

Directions: Four blocks east of Wadsworth Blvd. on Colfax Ave. (15th Ave.).

LAKEWOOD

Adolph Coors is buried at Crown Hill Cemetery in Lakewood (8500 W. 29th Ave., (303) 233-4611). The beer magnate committed suicide in a Virginia hotel in 1929.

Which is larger, the diner or the sign?

Davies' Chuck Wagon Diner

There are painfully few classic diners left in the Denver area, and none of them holds a candle to Davies' Chuck Wagon Diner on West Colfax. Aficionados recognize it as a 1957 Mountain View (#516), but others just think of it as the place with the horse standing on the roof. It's hard to miss either way

with its three-story cowboy sign. Maintained in mint condition, the diner has been honored with a spot on the National Register of Historic Places.

9495 W. Colfax, Lakewood, CO 80215

(303) 237-5252

Hours: Daily 6:30 A.M.–3 P.M.

Cost: $4–$8

Directions: Two blocks east of Kipling St. on W. Colfax Ave.

Littleton
Alferd Packer's Grave

Under pressure from editors of the *Denver Post,* and its crusading reporter Polly Pry, the Colorado governor pardoned convicted cannibal Alferd Packer (see page 138) in 1901. On leaving prison, Alferd Packer swore off meat forever and became a vegetarian. He moved to Denver where he worked as a security guard for (you guessed it!) the *Denver Post.* In 1907, he collapsed from an epileptic fit in Deer Creek Canyon, near the Cash Ranch. He was cared for by two women who said he rambled on about his innocence until he expired on April 23.

When you visit Packer's grave, you'll notice that Alferd's headstone reads Alfred. Whether that was a mistake is anyone's guess. One theory on his unique name is that Alferd couldn't spell, and that his real name was Alfred. The other theory was that Alferd's parents couldn't spell, and made the same mistake. Whatever the case, the stonecutter changed it, and the headstone is incorrect. Alferd was buried beneath a concrete slab to discourage grave robbers.

Littleton Cemetery, Section 3, Lot 65, Grave #8, 6155 S. Prince, Littleton, CO 80120

(303) 794-0373

Hours: Daylight

Cost: Free

www.findagrave.com/cgi-bin/fg.cgi?page=gr&GRid=785

Directions: East of Santa Fe Dr., just south of Arapaho Community College.

MORRISON

The Beatles played their first Colorado concert at Red Rocks in 1964.

Morrison
Ad Coors's Kidnapping Site

The kidnapping of Adolph "Ad" Coors III was a shock to many in this small town where *nobody* messed with the Coors family or their beer empire. But somebody did. On February 9, 1960, the 44-year-old father of four disappeared on his way to work in Golden. His station wagon was found three miles from town on a wooden bridge over Turkey Creek, its keys in the ignition and its engine still running. Human blood, eyeglasses, and a tan cap were found at the scene. A ransom letter arrived from Denver the next day demanding a half million dollars.

The Coors family was ready to pay the ransom, but the call never came, probably because Ad was already dead. Witnesses helped police trace a mysterious car's license plate back to 1435 Pearl Street, Apartment 305, in Denver, home of Walter Osborne. Osborne had quickly departed the day after the kidnapping. His car was found burning in an Atlantic City dump a week later. The FBI matched fingerprints from the apartment to others in their files and discovered Osborne was really Joseph Corbett, Jr., an escaped murderer.

Ad Coors's body turned up in Douglas County on September 11, 1960, near an illegal dump. Police believe he had been shot twice in the back, probably at the original crime scene. The FBI ran a photo of Corbett in *Reader's Digest* in November and soon received some tips from Canada. Corbett was apprehended in Vancouver on October 29; he had been living under the name Thomas Wainwright. He was convicted of Coors's murder and sent to Cañon City for life.

Turkey Creek Canyon Rd., Morrison, CO 80465

No phone

Hours: Always visible

Cost: Free

Directions: Head west on Rte. 285, turn south on Turkey Creek Canyon Rd. (Rte. 122), go to the bridge of the creek.

WHEATRIDGE

Wheatridge claims to be "The Carnation Capital of the World."

Tiny Town . . . or KING KONG KIDS!!??!?
Photo by author, courtesy of Tiny Town

Tiny Town

This is what happens when a hobby gets out of hand. In 1915, George Turner started building Tiny Town's first home as a playhouse for his daughter. By 1920 the project had expanded and was opened to tourists. Originally known as Turner's Tiny Town, it quickly became a favorite of Denver-area children. In 1939, a coal-fired, kid-size railroad started hauling passengers around the collection of small-scale buildings.

But nothing good lasts forever, and the park eventually closed. During the 1970s and 1980s, floods, fires, and vandals laid waste to many of the original structures. In 1988, a group of civic-minded people rebuilt and restored the town to its original splendor. The project was funded by Tiny Town fans who "bought" lots and property, though it might have been more realistic had the tiny people moved in. Now you can once again explore the more than 100 buildings in this handcrafted village, peeking in the windows like a giant voyeur. Try to imagine what it would be like to be Godzilla or King Kong, bringing chaos and fear to this little hamlet. It's every child's fantasy.

6249 S. Turkey Creek Rd., Morrison, CO 80465

(303) 697-6829

Hours: June–August, daily 10 A.M.–5 P.M.; May, September–October, Saturday–Sunday 10 A.M.–5 P.M.

Cost: Adults $3, Kids (2–12) $2; Train $1

www.tinytownrailroad.com

Directions: South off Rte. 285 at Turkey Creek Rd.

Eastern Colorado
and the Front Range

*I*t must have been disappointing for settlers heading west, as it is for travelers today, to cross into Colorado from Nebraska or Kansas and expect to see the gold-rich mountains on the horizon ahead. Instead, the state's eastern plains offer more barren flatness, not so much as a bump to be seen. Zero. Zilch. Nada. The big goose egg.

But not so fast . . . what the area lacks in topography it more than makes up for in strangeness. Filling stations made out of petrified wood. Evening gowns stitched together from rattlesnake skins. Stone giants cast from Portland cement. They can all be found in communities on the state's eastern plains and front range.

The desolate and often inhospitable region has also been the site of some of the state's most deadly tragedies, like the Sand Creek Massacre, the Towner bus accident, the bombing of Flight 629, the Flagler Air Show disaster, the burning of Julesburg, and the Ludlow Massacre. With a few exceptions, each of these carnage sites are marked and open to the public, so bring those cameras—it's time to have some fun!

Beulah
The Solid Muldoon

Many interesting fossils have been unearthed in Colorado, but none has been as jaw-dropping as the petrified giant found near Beulah on September 16, 1877. Discovered by William A. Conant, the 7.5-foot humanoid known as the Solid Muldoon was not merely a pile of bones, but the whole darn body! Conant found it half-buried in an arroyo west of Pueblo, tangled in the roots of a cedar tree. In the process of extracting the giant, he broke off its head, revealing crystallized neck vertebrae.

The Solid Muldoon had a two-inch curled tail, long arms, and feet like an ape. Speculators immediately proclaimed it to be Darwin's missing link. It was put on display in a Pueblo theater (since torn down) at the southwest corner of Second Street and Santa Fe Avenue. One of the first people to visit it was none other than P. T. Barnum, which raised the suspicion of local reporters. Their visit to the supposed excavation site cast even more doubt on Conant's story, as neither a large cedar nor a large hole was found.

Barnum reportedly paid $15,000 for a 75-percent interest in the fossil, but it was later learned that it was not the first time he'd shelled out money for the Solid Muldoon. A few years earlier he had been contacted by George Hull of upstate New York, the man who had perpetrated the Cardiff Giant Hoax of 1869. Hull had built a new and improved giant that he planned to ship west to be "found." Barnum helped finance the construction and shipping of the 600-pound creation to Colorado; then he made sure he could be nearby when it was unveiled. The Solid Muldoon eventually landed at Barnum's New York Museum of Anatomy, where it attracted thousands of paying customers a day. Soon after, one unpaid conspirator in the plot, E. J. Cox, revealed the whole scam.

If you want to see where this petrified missing link was "found," look two-thirds up the side of Muldoon Hill on the south side of the road east of Beulah. The Beulah Historical Society erected a fake tombstone along Route 78, just east of Siloam Road, on July 22, 1984, for the benefit of the History Channel's *In Search of History* program.

Excavation Site, Rte. 78, Beulah, CO 81023

No phone

Hours: Always visible

Cost: Free

Directions: Seven miles northeast of Beulah on Rte. 78, on the south side of the road.

Boulder
Spacey Town

Calling Boulder a Spacey Town is not intended as a slam against its reputation as a home for old hippies and crunchy outdoor types. It's just hard to escape the historical fact that this front-range community has had more than its fair share of cosmic residents and events.

First off, astronaut M. Scott Carpenter was born in Boulder on May 1, 1925, and eventually attended the University of Colorado. Carpenter became the fourth American in outer space after blasting off from Cape Canaveral on May 24, 1962. His hometown has honored the Mercury astronaut with a public park, complete with a rocket-shaped jungle gym and slide.

Scott Carpenter Park, 30th St. and Arapaho Ave., Boulder, CO 80303

No phone

Hours: Daily 6 A.M.–10 P.M.

Cost: Free

Directions: Two blocks east of 28th St. (Rte. 36), just south of the Crossroads Mall.

The University of Colorado has another space cowboy alum: Marshall Herff Applewhite, eventual leader of Heaven's Gate. Long before he and 38 followers rode off on the Hale-Bopp Comet, he studied music at the University of Colorado at Boulder. Applewhite played the lead in campus productions of *Oklahoma!* and *South Pacific.*

University Theatre, University of Colorado at Boulder, Campus Box 261, Boulder, CO 80309

(303) 492-6309

Hours: Always visible

Cost: Free

www.colorado.edu/TheatreDance/

Directions: Just northeast of the intersection of College Ave. and Broadway.

Applewhite likely discounted the university's most infamous research project: the 1966–1968 Condon Committee. Funded by the U.S. Air Force and headed by astrophysics professor Dr. Edward U. Condon, it was formed to investigate the possibility of UFOs.

Condon was hardly open-minded regarding the subject, which was just fine with Air Force brass. He often referred to UFOs as "goof-ohs" and was once quoted as saying, ". . . there's nothing to [UFO sightings], but I'm not supposed to reach a conclusion for another year." The Condon Committee, it turns out, was more interested in debunking suspicious sightings than investigating them. Several staff members quit or were fired after refusing to participate in what they felt was a cover-up.

The committee's final report was used to justify the Air Force's decision to cancel Project Bluebook. UFOs were explained away as nothing more than swamp gas, seagulls, temperature inversions, and hallucinations.

Department of Astrophysical and Planetary Sciences, LASP Space Technology Building, Campus Box 391, University of Colorado at Boulder, Boulder, CO 80309
(303) 492-8915
Hours: Always visible
Cost: Free
aps.colorado.edu/index.html
Directions: North of Colorado Ave. on Discovery Dr.

Alien life forms became a joke in Spacey Town, especially after Mork arrived from Ork. The 1970s sitcom *Mork and Mindy*—a spin-off of *Happy Days*—was set in then-present-day Boulder. If you've forgotten (and lucky you, if you have!) Mork lived with Mindy and worked at the New York Deli (1117 Pearl Street, since closed).

The owners of Mindy's house have not been enthusiastic about their association with the creative vehicle that launched Robin Williams's career (and the rainbow suspender fad). They once hung up a sign announcing, "Mork doesn't live here, SO GO AWAY!" Mork's apartment was located on the second floor, in the room with the bay window.

Mork and Mindy's Home (McCallister House), 1619 Pine St., Boulder, CO 80302
Private phone
Hours: Always visible, view from street
Cost: Free
Directions: Four blocks north of Canyon Blvd. at 16th St.

Tea Time

Celestial Seasonings is one of those hippie hobby-turned-million-dollar enterprises that are not uncommon in Boulder. It all started in the late 1960s when teenager Mo Siegal began hiking around the mountains near Aspen, picking herbs and digging up roots to make a special brew. Originally, the tea was for his own consumption, but while living in Boulder in 1970, Siegal joined forces with Wyck Hay to produce the first batch of Mo's 36 Herb Tea, hand-sewn muslin bags crammed with every tasty weed the hills had to offer.

It was a hit, and the pair soon followed it with Red Zinger, Sleepytime, and so on, until they became the nation's largest producer of herbal teas. And how things have changed, as you'll see on the tour. All those hippie locks are tucked under hair nets, and the herbs are processed, bagged, and packaged by machines. The vaguely trippy artwork that appears on the boxes is created on computers, as you'll see in the art department. And judging by the slick marketing in the gift shop, these folks have learned a thing or two since their flower-power days.

Celestial Seasonings, 4600 Sleepytime Dr., Boulder, CO 80301

(303) 581-1202

Tour Hours: Monday–Saturday 10 A.M.–3 P.M., Sunday 11 A.M.–3 P.M.; Celestial Cafe, Monday–Friday 7–10 A.M., 11 A.M.–2 P.M.

Cost: Free

www.celestialseasonings.com

Directions: East of Foothills Pkwy., three blocks north of Jay Rd.

BENNETT

Colorado's highest recorded temperature was 118°F on July 11, 1888, in Bennett.

BETHUNE

Actor **Denver Pyle** was born in Bethune on May 11, 1920.

BURLINGTON

You may not smoke a pipe after sunset on the streets of Burlington.

Eeeeeekkkk!

Photo by author, courtesy of the Kit Carson County Carousel

Burlington
Kit Carson County Carousel

Have you ever ridden a giraffe with a snake twisted around its neck? How about a zebra . . . while a gnome tries to jab your ass with a spear? Don't feel bad—few people have, unless they've taken a spin on the Kit Carson County Carousel.

This small community's carousel was built in 1905 by the Philadelphia

Toboggan Company for Denver's Elitch Gardens. It was the sixth ride the company ever built, and it is the only one that still has its original paint, which is why the ride is sometimes called The Jewel of America and is listed as a National Historic Landmark. The town of Burlington bought the used carousel in 1928 for $1,200. The county commissioners who approved the purchase were run out of office during the Depression for their extravagant purchase, but time has vindicated their decision.

The carousel has 46 characters, including giraffes, deer with real antlers, chariots, long-horned goats, a saddled St. Bernard, and a hippocampus—sort of a half-horse, half-seahorse mutant. Many of the carved creatures are embellished with snakes, monkeys, and gnomes. Because the characters are stationary, the carousel can spin at the breakneck speed of 12 MPH, as opposed the standard 8 MPH of jumper carousels. Round and round you'll go, all to the blaring tunes of an original Wurlitzer Monster Military Band Organ.

Kit Carson County Fairgrounds, 17th St. & Colorado Ave., Burlington, CO 80807

Contact: Kit Carson County Carousel, Inc., PO Box 28, Stratton, CO 80836

(719) 346-8070

Hours: June–August, daily 1–8 P.M.; September–May, by appointment

Cost: Adults $2.50

www.carousel.net/org/kcc/KCCarousel.htm

Directions: Six blocks north of Rte. 24 on 14th St., just north of the railroad tracks; follow the signs to the fairgrounds.

CASTLE ROCK

Castle Rock could have been named Pound Cake. Explorer **John Charles Frémont** named it that on maps during his first visit to the area.

Geologists have discovered a ridge near Castle Rock that had been struck by lightning 120,000 times over a period of several years.

Chivington
Sand Creek Massacre

In the long, sad history of the U.S. government's treatment of Native Americans during the westward expansion, the Sand Creek Massacre stands out as one of the nation's most despicable chapters. Certainly, it is Colorado's worst.

The tragic sequence of events seems to have started by an unprovoked settler attack on the Cheyenne chief Lean Bear in May 1864. Lean Bear was killed, and soon tensions were riding high on the eastern plains. Chief Motavato, better known as Black Kettle, urgently told Colorado's territorial governor, John Evans, that the Cheyenne didn't want war. But Arapaho warriors raided the homestead of the four-member Hungate family near present-day Parker on June 11. The Hungate Massacre—Ward Hungate was shot 80 times—solidified anti-Indian sentiment in Denver, especially after the Hungates' bodies were brought to Denver and put on public display. Colonel John Chivington, who was known as the fighting parson, was put in command of the Third Colorado Volunteers, a militia of 725 with a simple mandate: to kill hostile Indians.

Governor Evans ordered all peaceful Cheyennes to go to Fort Lyon to get provisions and to avoid angry settlers. But Evans had an ulterior motive. Once the Cheyenne arrived, fort commander Major Edward Wynkoop was ordered to escort them to Big Sandy Creek, 40 miles away. Wynkoop was thought to be sympathetic to the Cheyenne, and once he returned, was relieved of duty.

Soon, Chivington's "Bloodless" Third (they had yet to engage in battle) arrived at Fort Lyon. The colonel announced, "I have come to kill Indians, and believe it is right and honorable to use any means under God's heaven to kill Indians." And they did just that, on November 29, 1864.

Black Kettle's camp had 500 Cheyenne; about two-thirds were women, children, and elderly people. At dawn, the cavalry fired on the camp. Black Kettle had everyone rush to stand under his American flag, along with a white surrender flag. He had been given the flag by Indian Commissioner A. B. Greenwood with the assurance that as long as the American flag was raised, no harm would come to his people. Yet the flags just made the Cheyenne an easier target. Militia raced in and cut open expectant mothers, cut scalps and genitals from men and women, shot children, and left infants to die on the prairie. "Nits make lice!" shouted Chivington.

The militia headed home with their gruesome trophies strung over their saddle horns. Had most of the volunteers not been drunk, more Cheyenne might have died, and more of their own might have lived (only nine militiamen perished, but 28 more were wounded). Most of the wounded soldiers' injuries were due to the fact that the militiamen were firing from opposite sides of the encampment.

Chivington bragged they'd killed 400 to 500 warriors, but it was more like 28 men and 105 women and children. Chivington and his men received a victory parade in Denver. When details of what actually happened began to emerge, Congress began an investigation. Before Chivington could be court-martialed, he resigned his position. Governor Evans was also forced to resign.

Miraculously, Black Kettle survived the attack, and signed a peace treaty a year later. A lot of good it did him; four years later in November 1868, George Armstrong Custer and the Seventh Cavalry ambushed Black Kettle's surviving tribe along the Washita River, and killed them all.

Chivington is the closest town to the Sand Creek Massacre site which, until you see the place, sounds like adding insult to injury. But Chivington appears to have been laid to waste by vengeful elements. Barely a building is left standing. The National Park Service is now in the process of erecting an accurate, appropriate monument on the site.

County Road 54 & W Road, Chivington, CO 81036

No phone

Hours: Always visible

Cost: Free

Directions: Four miles north of Rte. 96 along Big Sandy Creek.

EVANS

Between 20 and 100 kernels of corn fell every day on a 50-square-foot plot of ground along Pleasant Acres Drive in Evans, beginning in 1987. Corn continues to fall, though less frequently. Sometimes, residents find pinto beans.

Flagler's ready.

Flagler
Don't Mess with Flagler!

You can't blame these Flagler folk for being a little edgy; they've been attacked from the skies before. On September 15, 1951, the town was hosting an air show. Spectators were lined up in cars at the football field, watching the acrobatics, when one of the stunt pilots lost control of his aircraft and plowed into the crowd. In all, 19 people and the pilot died, which especially considering the town's population, was a tremendous blow.

But today Flagler is prepared for any incoming air attack. A TM-76 Mace cruise missile has been erected in the town park. (There's a monument to the air show accident victims in the same park.) The missile's nose cone points southeast to greet the rising sun and travelers exiting from Interstate 70. This town may be small, but it's armed to the teeth.

Ruffner Ave. & 2nd St., Flagler, CO 80815

No phone

Hours: Always visible

Cost: Free

Directions: In the park at the southeast end of town, north of I-70.

Feel free to sing along.
Photo by author, courtesy of Pat Lundreth and Suzanne Montando

Fort Collins
The Bungled Jungle

Whatever cosmic force brought Pat Lundreth and Suzanne Montando into contact with Bill Swets is anyone's guess, but we're all the richer for it. This unashamedly goofy couple has built an elaborate, creature-filled wonderland inside the outbuildings of the already fantabulous Swetsville Zoo, allowing you to appreciate two unique art environments within one stop!

The Bungled Jungle features hundreds of full-size papier-mâché figures gathered together in a dozen or so pseudo-museum dioramas. One shows aliens out for a spin in their rocket-propelled cruiser, another is a subterranean cavern populated by lanky troglodytes, and the next has a green-skinned Martian rock band playing funky instruments. The figures are painted in bright fluorescent colors and clothed in thrift-shop throwaways, fake jewelry, and feather boas.

Lundreth and Montando are full-time artists and full-time free spirits. Try to catch them during one of the weekends they're having an art show. For a reasonable price you can adopt a Bungled Jungle critter to bring home.

4819 E. Harmony Rd., Fort Collins, CO 80528

Contact: PO Box 367, Tinmath, CO 80547

(970) 493-6309

E-mail: contact@bungledjungle.com

Hours: Daily 9 A.M.–5 P.M.

Cost: Free

www.bungledjungle.com

Directions: Inside the buildings at the Swetsville Zoo (see page 51).

FORT COLLINS

Fort Collins has proclaimed itself "The Safest Spot on Earth." However, a local Catholic priest pushed an 18-year-old tambourine player down a flight stairs in 1983 because she played "the same way over and over again!"

Supreme Court Associate **Justice Byron "Whizzer" White** was born in Fort Collins on June 8, 1917.

Two heads are better than one.
Photo by author, courtesy of Bill Swets

The Swetsville Zoo

This isn't a zoo in the traditional sense—there are no cages or fences—but don't worry. None of the 120 creatures in this menagerie are alive . . . they're metal! Farmer/welder/artist Bill Swets began tinkering with leftover car parts and farm machinery more than 15 years ago in an attempt to make a bird sculpture to rival one he'd seen at a friend's home.

He succeeded. Today, the Swetsville Zoo has a two-headed dragon, a rocket-powered turtle, an Elvis alligator, a Tammy Faye flamingo, a Volkswagen spider, a musical trumpet swan, and lots of rusty dinosaurs. The zoo is landscaped with metal flowers and spinning windmills along a winding path that hugs the Poudre River.

And what's that castle you see at the zoo? That's Bill and wife Sandy's home, also known as the Mini Taj. It had to be rebuilt a few years back after a zoo visitor burned it down with a carelessly tossed cigarette. Back behind the Mini Taj somewhere is a converted city bus called Bill and Sandy's Dream Machine, used for road trips, complete with a queen-size bed.

4801 E. Harmony Rd., Fort Collins, CO 80528

(970) 484-9509

Hours: Daylight

Cost: Free; donations accepted

Directions: Just east of I-25, Exit 265, at Harmony Rd. (Rte. 68).

NOT QUITE PEARL HARBOR

When he was 10 years old, Bill Swets witnessed the Japanese bombing . . . of Tinmath! During the final years of World War II, the Japanese released 9,300 *fu-go* balloons laden with incendiary bombs into the Pacific jet stream. The intention was to ignite forest fires across the western United States, but only 300 or so ever made it far enough, and those did little damage. One *fu-go* landed on the Tinmath farm of John Swets, Bill's father, on March 19, 1945. It blasted a four-foot-deep crater in a field.

FORT LUPTON

Music listeners who violate Fort Lupton's noise ordinances are likely to be sentenced to listen to an hour of Barney, Barry Manilow, and bagpipes by Judge Paul Sacco. Or they can pay a $65 fine. The judge's strategy has a 0 percent recidivism rate.

FORT MORGAN

Large parts of Log Lane Village remain northwest of Fort Morgan (along Route 144, north of I-76). When it was established, all buildings had to be made of logs—or at least look like they were—and the streets were named after trees. The zoning rule was rescinded in the 1960s.

Fort Morgan
Glenn Miller's Early Days

Though he was born in Clarinda, Iowa, and spent a few years in North Platte, Nebraska, and Grant City, Missouri, Glenn Miller always considered Colorado home. In 1918, when Glenn was 14, his family loaded themselves and all their belongings into a railroad boxcar and headed west.

Glenn had already gotten a taste for music in Grant City. He began by playing the mandolin, but exchanged that for a trombone—in retrospect, a pretty smart trade. Miller's father worked as a handyman at the old Fort Morgan High School (300 Lake Street, now torn down) where Glenn was a student from 1918 to 1922.

Though hardly a model student, in football Glenn was All-State left end in 1920. And of course, his trombone playing wasn't bad, either. This earned him the nickname Johnnie Pumphandle . . . or at least that's how the locals say he got it. Miller practiced all the time, often annoying students, teachers, neighbors, siblings—anyone with ears. To find a secluded place to play, he climbed onto the high school roof one evening. He was later arrested.

The Miller family rented several homes in Fort Morgan: 508 West Street (torn down), 202 Maple Street (still standing), and 318 Prospect Street (still standing). After Glenn became a successful bandleader, he bought his mother a home at 825 Lake Street (still standing). Glenn Miller enlisted in the Army Air Corps during World War II. He disappeared over the English Channel on December 15, 1944, while flying to Paris to set up a Christmas concert. He was 39 years old. The memorial flag that flew at Arlington, and would have flown over his body had anyone found it, is in the town's historical museum.

Fort Morgan Museum, 414 Main St., PO Box 184, Fort Morgan, CO 80701

(970) 867-6331

E-mail: ftmormus@ftmorganmus.org

Hours: Monday–Friday 10 A.M.–5 P.M., Tuesday–Thursday 6–8 P.M., Saturday 11 A.M.–5 P.M.

Cost: Free

www.ftmorganmus.org

Directions: Two blocks south of Rte. 34, in the same building as the Fort Morgan Library.

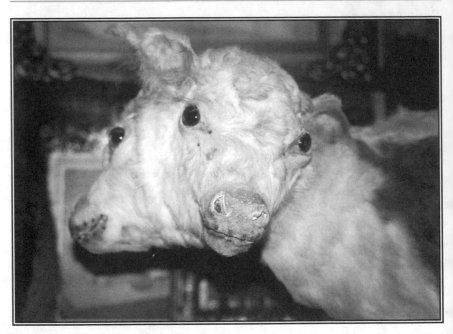

Two heads are *not always* better than one.
Photo by author, courtesy of the Wonder View Tower

Genoa
Wonder View Tower

"SEE 6 STATES!" the sign screams. Just climb the 87 steps to what the 1934 Geological Survey confirmed to be "the highest point between New York and Denver," and you're supposed to be able to see Colorado, Wyoming, Nebraska, South Dakota, Kansas, and New Mexico. But even if you believe this bold claim, you need a clear day to see much more than Colorado and Kansas from atop this 65-foot tower, and then the question is . . . "Why?" With so much wonderful stuff *inside* the Wonder View Tower, why would you waste your time looking for these flat states *outside*?

Wonder View Tower was built in the 1930s by C. W. Gregory and Myrtle le Bow. The inside is encrusted with rocks embedded into cement and more than 1,000 paintings by Princess Raven Wing. Mind you, these aren't just any rocks, but rocks collected from every state in the nation! The hike up the tower steps is more interesting than the view. The walls in the stairways are covered in paint-by-number landscapes and other thrift shop art. You pass through one dinky room after another to see tables stacked high with chipped china, telephone insulators, wooden carvings, discarded signs, jars filled with bottle caps, camel nose rings, branding irons, fish fossils, arrowheads arranged in frames—you name it—and no fewer than 50,000 antique bottles (and they're all for sale!).

What's more, your visit will be educational: scattered throughout the museum are more than 300 "Guess What's" where owner/curator/tour guide Jerry Chubbock prods you, "Do you know what that's used for?" If you answer enough of the questions correctly, he'll refund your $1 admission. The questions turn out to be tougher than Regis Philbin ever asks (unless you grew up on a ranch 100 years ago), and the payoff is $999,999 less.

Be sure to ask to see the stuffed two-headed calf, tucked away in a far corner. A half-dozen jars surround the mutation, each with a different animal oddity inside. Sadly, the formaldehyde evaporated or leaked out years ago, leaving mummified critters covered in dust and resting in the bottoms of the bottles. Chubbock makes an out-loud mental note: "I gotta refill those someday."

30121 Frontage Rd., Genoa, CO 80818

(719) 763-2309

Hours: March–September, daily 8 A.M.–8 P.M.; October–February, call ahead

Cost: Adults $1, Kids (12–17) 50¢

Directions: Exit 371 from I-70, follow the frontage road 0.5 miles west to the tower.

Granada
The Ghost of Camp Ameche

In recent years we have been reminded of the unconstitutional internment of Japanese Americans during World War II. Most of the victims of this government-organized witch hunt were from the West Coast, yet many were displaced as far from their homes as this facility in eastern Colorado, Camp Ameche. Almost 8,000 people were detained here starting in September 1942; it was the only such camp located in the state.

The 11,000-acre Camp Ameche had farms where prisoners raised their own vegetables and cattle. Today, all that's left are some concrete foundations, rattlesnakes, a monument to 31 men who volunteered for duty and were killed in action, and a ghost. One of the many people who died while imprisoned in the camp was a Japanese American socialite; some claim she was of royal blood. Still angry about her less-than-noble end, her long-cloaked figure has been spotted wandering the grounds.

Rte. 23.5 & FF Rd., Granada, CO 81041

No phone

Hours: Always visible

Cost: Free

Directions: Approximately 0.8 miles west of town on Rte. 50, south on Rte. 23.5, a half
mile to the gate.

Greeley
Rattlesnake Kate's Dress

It was a scene out of *Indiana Jones*. Kate Slaughterback and her three-year-old son Ernie stumbled into a rattlesnake den on October 28, 1925, near her farm east of Ione. Slaughterback was lucky enough to have a .22 Remington rifle with her—she was looking for ducks wounded by local hunters—when she ran across the first rattlesnake. She shot it, and another couple appeared. She shot them as well. Snakes continued to appear long past the time when she ran out of ammo. Slaughterback clubbed the serpents with the butt of the gun and the post from a "No Hunting" sign. When it was over two hours later, she'd killed 140 rattlers, enough to fill three washtubs.

The event became known as the Battle of Rattlesnake Hill, and Kate used the skinned vipers to make a dress, headband, shoes, and a rattle necklace she'd wear to local parades and dances. Riding her fame as a snake killer, she sold mounted snakes to visitors, and kept cages of the vipers behind her home. Slaughterback died in 1969 and was buried at the Mizpah Cemetery in Platteville. Her tombstone reads "Rattlesnake Kate." The famous rattlesnake dress, newly restored, hangs in the collection of Centennial Village in Greeley.

Centennial Village, 1475 A St., Greeley, CO 80631

(970) 350-9220

E-mail: dillc@ci.greeley.co.us

Hours: April–May, September–October, Tuesday–Saturday 10 A.M.–3 P.M.; June–August,
Tuesday–Saturday, 10 A.M.–5 P.M.

Cost: Adults $3.50, Seniors $3, Kids (6–12) $2

www.ci.greeley.co.us/culture/museums.html

Directions: Northwest of downtown at 14th and A Sts.

Puny prison.

Haswell
America's Smallest Jail

The Haswell Jail claims to be the smallest pokey in the United States, and though you don't have to be a Munchkin to be incarcerated there, it helps. It was built in 1921 and measures 10 by 12 feet. The outer wall is concrete, reinforced from within by steel. The jail is still in fairly good shape, but hasn't been used for years because of a little problem: somebody lost the key. No matter, there's barely anyone left in this plains community to lock up.

3rd & Main Sts., Haswell, CO 81045

No phone

Hours: Always visible

Cost: Free

Directions: Just west of Main St. on 3rd St., south of the playground.

Holly
As Low As You Can Go

It's all you hear: Rocky Mountain High! Rocky Mountain High! Blah, blah, blah. Sure, Colorado has three-quarters of the nation's land over 10,000 feet, 54 mountains over 14,000 feet, and the nation's highest average elevation at 6,800 feet.

But what about Rocky Mountain *Low*??!?! Where's that?

Holly, that's where. Sitting on the floodplain of the Arkansas River as it dumps into Kansas, Holly is the lowest town in a very high state. But although it is the bottom by Colorado standards (at 3,397 feet) it's still the highest low point of any state in the country. What's more, even the lowest point in Holly is higher than every point in Alabama, Arkansas, Connecticut, Delaware, Florida, Illinois, Indiana, Iowa, Louisiana, Maryland, Michigan, Minnesota, Mississippi, Missouri, New Jersey, Ohio, Pennsylvania, Rhode Island, and Wisconsin. So there.

City Clerk of Holly, 413 W. Cheyenne, Holly, CO 81047

(719) 537-6622

Hours: Always visible

Cost: Free

Directions: All over town.

HASTINGS
An explosion at a Hastings coal mine on April 27, 1917, killed 121 miners.

HEADSTRONG
The town of Headstrong was created when not-so-happy grocer Cleve Mason moved his store from Happyville, two miles away. Happyville has, sadly, disappeared.

HOLLY
An image of the Virgin of Guadalupe appeared on the bedroom wall of a Holly woman in 1997. She now has it covered by glass with a frame glued to the wall.

Not a good place to land in the ditch.

The Towner Bus Tragedy

Most adults remember snow days fondly: time off school to sled, build snowmen, and enjoy the winter weather. But a few folks from Holly have nightmares. They are the 15 surviving students of the Towner bus tragedy.

A blizzard hit the eastern plains on March 26, 1931, yet Pleasant Hill Elementary hadn't canceled classes until after bus driver Carl Miller showed up with his load. Miller tried to take a shortcut to get the kids back to their homes, but the bus ran off the road a mile north of the school. Thinking he could make it back to get help, he left the children and set off on foot. Due to whiteout conditions, he became lost and eventually froze to death.

Back at the bus, the children were getting cold. A window had been broken in the accident, and the snow was blowing in. To keep warm, the kids burned their school books and huddled in a corner. Before their parents found the bus 31 hours later, five of the children had died of hypothermia. Student Bryan Untiedt, credited with keeping the young children calm during the ordeal, was hailed as a hero. President Herbert Hoover invited him to the White House for a visit.

Today, a stone monument marks where the bus hit the ditch 70 years ago.

Holly–Towner Rd., Holly, CO 81047

No phone

Hours: Always visible

Cost: Free

Directions: Head north on First St., which turns into Holly–Towner Rd. (35 Rd., and jogs over to 37 Rd.); drive 18 miles; the monument is on the west side of the road.

Ah, the good-ol', bad-ol' days!

Iliff
Pump It!

Ah, the good ol' days! Smallpox . . . no TV . . . pumping your water at the town well . . . no wonder people get nostalgic! If you want to get an idea of

the way things were, either because your memory is slipping or because you're too young to know any better, stop by the tiny village of Iliff. Smack in the middle of the town's main intersection is the old town pump. People who keep track of such things believe it to be the only town pump remaining in Colorado.

Today the pump is protected by a small shed designed to keep drivers from slamming into this old-time oddity. But why was this road hazard never removed? Perhaps it's because Iliff has bigger projects to worry about—like someday paving their streets.

3rd Ave. & 4th St., Iliff, CO 80736

No phone

Hours: Always visible

Cost: Free

Directions: Just east of the post office (401 W. 3rd St.).

KIT CARSON

The community of Kit Carson once had to be burned to the ground because of a rat infestation.

After becoming the German chancellor, **Adolf Hitler** ended up with a mortgage note on 12,300 acres of ranch land near Kit Carson, and was therefore the owner. When the United States declared war on Germany, the land was impounded by the federal government.

LA JUNTA

A couple spotted several blond aliens in blue jumpsuits near La Junta in the summer of 1975. They emerged from a UFO shaped like an elongated donut.

Legendary lawman **Bat Masterson** was marshall of La Junta in 1884 and served only five weeks.

Julesburg
Ears to Jules Beni!

Mark Twain once called Julesburg "The Wickedest City in the West," and did he ever get that one right! Founded by a criminal and nearly wiped out three times by justifiably hostile Indians and greedy rail barons, it's amazing there is anything left to see.

Julesburg was cursed from the start. Horse thief Jules Beni established this trading post in the 1850s, just south of present-day Ovid. Beni was hired by the Overland Stage Company as a station agent but was relieved of his duties in 1858 and replaced by Jack Slade. Overland officials suspected Beni had been involved in several inside robbery jobs. Beni did not take the accusations well, even though they were true, and took his revenge out on Slade; he shot his replacement 13 times.

Remarkably, Slade survived, and vowed to kill Beni. Who can blame him? While Slade was recovering from his wounds, the Overland superintendent arrived and ordered Beni hanged. The town's founder was strung up three different times, but the life was never choked out of him. Beni was released and ordered never to return.

But Slade wasn't going to let his attacker get away. A few years later, he tracked Beni near the Virginia Dale station. Slade's posse tied Beni to a post where Slade shot him point-blank and cut off both his ears. He nailed one ear to the door of the Pony Express station, and kept the other as a watch fob when he returned to Julesburg.

Slade was employed by the Overland for several years before being dismissed for excessive drinking and brawling. At the time, Julesburg had other problems to contend with. On February 2, 1865, 2,000 Cheyenne, Arapaho, and Sioux torched Julesburg. The settlers watched their town burn from within the protective walls of Fort Sedgwick (then called Fort Rankin). They rebuilt their town in 1866, several miles due east of the rubble, on the south side of the South Platte River. When the Union Pacific laid its tracks north of the river a year later, the town relocated to a spot near Weir Station. The Union Pacific established its own town six miles to the east in 1880, and named it Denver Junction. That town later was renamed Julesburg . . . for the fourth time.

Fort Sedgwick Depot Museum, 202 W. First Ave., Julesburg, CO 80737

(970) 474-2061

Hours: June–August, Monday–Saturday 9 A.M.–4:30 P.M., Sunday 1–4:30 P.M.
Cost: Adults $1, Kids 50¢
Directions: Four blocks west of the intersection of Rtes. 138 and 385.

Vanilla on the southern slope, chocolate on the northern.

Ice Cream Mountain

It can be a bit of a disappointment driving from the east into Colorado.
You've endured hundreds of miles of Iowa and Nebraska where hills, to
say nothing of the mountains, are a rarity. Then you cross the border to
find that Colorado, at least here, is as flat as where you came from. And

then you see it, a gigantic peak looming ahead, chocolatey brown with snow on its southern slope . . .

Wait a second. *Southern* slope? That's no mountain. That's a huge ice cream cone—a Sweden Creme, no less! Alone beside I-76, this 12-foot-high homemade advertisement has been attracting westbound travelers for decades. Sweden Cone is only open during the summer, though the jumbo treat is visible all year long.

Sweden Creme, 15177 Rte. 385, RR1/PO Box 1A, Julesburg, CO 80737

(970) 474-2863

Hours: Restaurant open May–October, daily 11 A.M.–7 P.M.

Cost: Free

Directions: Just north of the Julesburg exit from I-76.

Lafayette
Anywhere but Utah

On November 21, 1927, six striking miners were killed by state militiamen at the Columbine Mine near Lafayette. Their bodies were laid out together in an unmarked grave at Lafayette Cemetery, covered over, and mostly forgotten.

Then, some 60-odd years later and 2,000 miles away, employees at the National Archives came across an envelope filled with ashes. They turned out to be the partial cremains of labor organizer Joe Hill. Remember the song? The Wobblie (International Workers of the World) had been railroaded for murder and put to death by a Utah firing squad in 1915, and his final request was that his ashes be scattered all across the United States . . . *but not in Utah!*

Meanwhile, plans were underway to erect a marker over the Columbine Mine victims' graves, and word got to Lafayette about the leader's ashes. With the blessing of the Hill family, Joe's cremains were scattered over the newly erected marker during dedication ceremonies in 1989.

Lafayette Cemetery, Rte. 287 & S. Boulder Rd., Lafayette, CO 80026

No phone

Hours: Always visible

Cost: Free

Directions: At the intersection of Rte. 287 and S. Boulder Rd., on the eastern edge of the cemetery.

A termite's nightmare.

Lamar
Petrified Wood Service Station
Though termites have never been a big problem in Colorado, W. G. Brown wasn't taking any chances. When he built his service station along Route 50 in 1932, the wood he used was 175 million years old—petrified

wood! The two largest pieces, the trunks used to frame the main door, weighed 3,200 pounds each. The rest of the pieces were smaller but were cemented together to form what today looks like a giant wooden iceberg.

Brown's filling station is no longer in business, but his magnificent creation survives. Currently it's a storage room for Stagner Tire. The station's appearance in Ripley's *Believe It or Not!* column is commemorated on a sign above the main window.

Stagner Tire, 501 N. Main St., Lamar, CO 81052

(719) 336-3462

Hours: Always visible

Cost: Free

Directions: At the corner of Main and Sherman Sts., six blocks north of the intersection of Rtes. 50 and 287.

Larkspur
Ghostly Bar Hound

Fred White won't give it a rest. Not long after the local cowboy died in 1993, his spirit moved in at the Spur of the Moment bar. For whatever reason, the ghost likes to mess with the employees and patrons at this establishment. People have reported having their ponytails yanked, their bar stools moved out from under them, and the TV channels switching without warning. White has never appeared during business hours, but several workers have spotted him while they were cleaning up after closing. He appears in formal cowboy attire, which means new blue jeans and a bandanna.

Spur of the Moment, 8885 Spruce Mountain Dr., Larkspur, CO 80118

(303) 681-2990

Hours: Monday–Saturday 11 A.M.–Midnight, Sunday Noon–9 P.M.

Cost: $4–$8

Directions: Just north of Perry Park Ave.

Longmont
The Plan Fails

John Gilbert Graham didn't much like his mother, Daisy King, but he thought she might be good for some quick cash. So on November 1, 1955, he packed his mother's suitcase with two dozen sticks of dynamite, drove her to Stapleton Field, paid the fee for exceeding baggage weight, and kissed her good-bye for the last time.

United Flight 629 for Portland exploded east of Longmont, killing all 44 aboard. The DC-6B crashed onto the Jack Heil farm, leaving two large craters. The 24-year-old Graham wasted no time trying to cash in the three insurance policies he'd taken out in her name, each costing 50 cents, while waiting at Stapleton. Because he had failed to get King's signature, he wasn't able to collect the estimated $37,500 he felt he was due. He did, however, attract the attention of the FBI.

Graham had worked in demolition in the military, had been implicated in a suspicious explosion at his family's failing restaurant, and had taken a recent interest in timing devices at his job at an electronics store. When the feds discovered Graham had purchased dynamite at a Kremmling hardware store days before, he confessed.

Though he ultimately pleaded not guilty by reason of insanity, then tried to recant his confession, he was convicted of the bombing and multiple murders. Graham walked into Cañon City's gas chamber on January 11, 1957, with a much clearer understanding of his impending fate than he had allowed his dear departed mother.

I-15 & Rte. 119, Longmont, CO 80504

No phone

Hours: Always visible

Cost: Free

Directions: Eight miles east of town, just east of I-25, between Rte. 119 and Rte. 66.

LAMAR

Before becoming a silent movie star, **Tom Mix** mixed drinks in a Lamar bar in 1906.

LAS ANIMAS

Kit Carson, the frontiersman once described as "rather below the medium height, with brown, curling hair, little or no beard, and a voice as soft and as gentle as a woman's" died on May 23, 1868, at Fort Lyon (south of Route 50 on Route 183) from a ruptured aneurysm in his lung. His wife died a month later, leaving seven orphans.

Ludlow
The Ludlow Massacre

It was a sad but not atypical day in American labor history. Following a seven-month strike by the United Mine Workers at the Colorado Fuel and Iron Company, John D. Rockefeller convinced the Colorado governor to send in the Colorado National Guard. The miners had been asking for a 10-percent raise, strict enforcement of mining laws, union recognition, and the right to *not* shop at the company store—talk about *radical!* Ninety-three-year-old Mother Jones helped organize the strikers but was soon thrown into a Trinidad jail without any formal charges against her.

Then, on April 20, 1914, the guardsmen fired machine guns at, and later set fire to, the strikers' tent city. Eleven children and two women died in a cellar as the tent above them burned. The site became known as the Death Pit. Five other adults were killed, along with one guardsman.

Nobody was ever made to answer for the murders. Today, a monument and picnic ground maintained by the United Mine Workers of America stands over the site. The Death Pit is still visible.

Tent Camp Site, Del Aqua Rd., Ludlow, CO 81082

(719) 846-7217 (Trinidad History Museum)

Hours: Always visible

Cost: Free

www.trinidadco.com

Directions: One mile west of Exit 27 from I-25, just before the railroad crossing.

PUEBLO

Dandelions may not grow, by law, in the city of Pueblo.

A cottonwood that stood on the 300 block of South Union Street in Pueblo was used to hang 14 different men during the city's early history. "Old Monarch" was cut down in 1883, but a cross-section has been preserved at the Old Pueblo Museum.

Buggies that approach one another must both turn right at the earliest moment in Pueblo.

Pueblo
Bridey Murphy

The whole story seemed almost too weird to believe. Through hypnosis, Pueblo tractor salesman Morey Bernstein stumbled on "proof" of human reincarnation. According to his book, *The Search for Bridey Murphy*, on November 29, 1952, Bernstein turned back the psychological clock of Ruth Simmons using a then-new process called regression, all in the comfort of his living room! Rather than stop when he got to her birth, he backed her up through an ethereal purgatory, and into the life of Bridget "Bridey" Murphy, an Irish woman from the early 1800s. Simmons related details of her life in Cork, Ireland: the school she attended, the jigs she danced, the man she married, and the details of how she died falling down a flight of stairs at age 66.

Bernstein's book was an overnight bestseller. At last—proof of reincarnation! Soon "Come as You Were" parties were all the rage, and a movie was hastily put together. But things began to unravel when journalists started looking for the real Bridey Murphy in genealogical records back in Ireland. They found no evidence of a Bridget Murphy born in Cork in 1798, no record of her 1864 death in Belfast, and no confirmation of any of the details of the years in between. The elementary school she attended never existed, no marriage record was discovered between her and Sean Brian Joseph McCarthy, a man who was never on the faculty of Queen's University (as she stated). What's more, Bridey consistently mispronounced Irish terms.

Things looked even more questionable when reporters discovered Ruth Simmons was actually an alias for Virginia Tighe. As a young girl in Chicago, according to the *Chicago American*, Tighe lived next to a woman named Bridey Murphy Corkell, and for a time was infatuated with Corkell's son. She also performed monologues for high school assemblies in an Irish brogue. *Time* magazine proclaimed Bernstein's work as "more Blarney than Bridey."

Was that the end of it? Hardly. Reporters from the *Denver Post* began investigating the investigators, and plenty of errors were discovered in the *Chicago American* piece. Like an early version of the JFK assassination, so much information was called into question, uncertainty was more common than solid facts. People divided into camps of believers and nonbelievers. Still, the enthusiasm surrounding the book has never died. Past-life regression remains a staple with hypnotists. Virginia (Tighe) Morrow died on July 12, 1995. There's no telling when she'll be back.

Morey Bernstein's Home/Hypnosis Site, 1819 Elizabeth St., Pueblo, CO 81003
Private phone
Hours: Always visible, view from street
Cost: Free
Directions: Two blocks west of Grand Ave., at Elizabeth and 18th Sts.

Virginia Tighe's Home, 925 Alexander Circle, Pueblo, CO 81001
Private phone
Hours: Always visible, view from street
Cost: Free
Directions: One block south of Bonforte Blvd., just east of Liberty Lane.

Star Nursery and Landscaping

Let's hear it for Star Nursery and Landscaping. While other landscaping companies stick to homes and businesses, Star has tackled an otherwise ugly piece of industrial land. Just south of the interchange of Route 50 and I-25, on the west side of the highway, is an enormous menagerie of fiberglass creatures. Full-size deer, elk, grizzlies, and a herd of antelope gaze out over the highway from atop piles of slag and railroad ties. Rising high above them all is a big white bronco on its hind legs, and we're not talking John Elway . . . it's a horse.

2006 N. Santa Fe Ave., Pueblo, CO 81003
(719) 543-1184
Hours: Always visible
Cost: Free
Directions: Just south of the Rte. 50 intersection with I-25, on the west side of the highway.

PUEBLO

On May 15, 1973, along Red Creek Road south of Pueblo, two teenage boys were harassed by a creature that looked like a haystack with glowing eyes. It has since been named the Wazooey Man.

One way to get to work on time.

Superplanes and Supertrains

The military/transportation museum at the Pueblo Memorial Airport is odd in that the trains it has on display are faster than most of the airplanes in its collection. It's not that the planes are clunkers; quite the contrary. But the trains are prototypes from the Department of Transportation's high-speed proving grounds east of town. If you've ever wanted to commute at speeds in excess of 300 MPH, check out the Garret Linear Induction Motor Research Vehicle, the Grumman Tracked Levitated Research Vehicle, or the Rohr Prototype Tracked Air Cushion Vehicle. You won't be late in one of these puppies, though you're likely to spill your coffee somewhere along the way.

The bulk of the museum collection consists of airplanes. Though it is also home to the International B-24 Memorial Museum, there is one item conspicuously lacking: a B-24! So many of these "Liberators" were lost in combat during World War II, almost none survive today, and those that have are expensive. You'll have to settle for the 20-some other planes and helicopters, both inside the hangar and outside on the fenced-in grounds.

The museum hangar is also filled with military memorabilia, including captured enemy armaments, uniforms, mess kits, swords, you name it. One of the most interesting displays is a collection of photographs of World War II nose-cone art. Every aircraft in the war had its own painted mascot, and though the artists varied, the theme remained relatively constant: bosomy dames. Nasty Nancy, Li'l De-icer, Milk Wagon Express, Daddy Please, Twin Niftys, Li'l Audrey Grows Up, Underexposed—you get the idea.

Pueblo Weisbrod Aircraft Museum/International B-24 Museum, 31001 Magnuson Ave., Pueblo, CO 81001

(719) 948-9219

Hours: Monday–Friday 10 A.M.–4 P.M., Saturday 10 A.M.–2 P.M., Sunday 1–4 P.M.

Cost: Adults $4, Kids (12 and under) Free

www.co.pueblo.co.us/pwam

Directions: Just north of Rte. 50 at the Rte. 233 intersection.

ROCKY FORD
Rocky Ford is "The Sweet Melon Capital of the World," and celebrates Watermelon Days each August.

SEDALIA
The nation's first U.S. forest ranger, **William Richard "Billy" Kreutzer**, hailed from Sedalia.

STERLING
Cats in Sterling must wear taillights.

World's Largest Mural

At 4.5 miles long and 60 feet high, the Pueblo Levee Mural Project is, by most accounts, the World's Largest Mural. It may also be the World's Most Toxic Mural.

The story begins on June 3, 1921, when the Arkansas River burst its banks, flooded the city, and drowned 132 Pueblo-area residents. When the waters subsided, the town built the Pueblo Levee to make sure it never happened again. For years the concrete-lined ditch was known as "The Black Hole of Pueblo," carrying away the sins of the city's steel mills to unfortunate towns downstream.

Clearly, the levee needed a makeover. City officials came up with an ingenious idea to use the paint collected from citizens during the annual Toxic Waste Day. Rather than dispose of the half-filled cans of paint, people were encouraged to use it to express themselves however they wished, profanity and gang symbols excluded, on the inner sloping surface of the levee. Thus was born the Pueblo Levee Mural Project.

Pueblo has recently rehabilitated the downtown stretch of the levee with the Historic Arkansas River Project (HARP), but its efforts are less toxic, more tasteful, and less populist. (The HARP cost around $24 million, whereas the PLMP was free.) You can still see remnants of the Pueblo Levee Mural, though it's fading.

Pueblo Levee Mural Project, Abriendo Ave., Pueblo, CO 81003

(800) 233-3446

Hours: Daylight hours

Cost: Free

www.pueblo.org

Directions: Start at the Fourth St. bridge and follow the levee.

Sedalia

Shamballa Ashrama and the Brotherhood of the White Temple

Built in 1946 in an "atom-proof" canyon on the Front Range (you heard right: no atoms!), the Brotherhood of the White Temple was originally intended to be a shelter from Armageddon. (Don't worry, the "white" refers only to the paint used.) The nuclear conflagration was to take place sometime in 1953, according to the Brotherhood's leader, Dr. Maurice

Doreal, nee Claude Doggins of Sulphur Springs, Oklahoma.

Of course, we're living proof that Dr. Doreal missed the mark on the end-of-the-world prediction. So where did he come up with his erroneous assertions? The answer is science fiction novels, the Bible, the pyramids, Nostradamus, Far East mysticism, and a wild imagination.

The Brotherhood of the White Temple was founded in 1930 when Doreal first revealed his knowledge of an Atlantean culture that lived deep inside northern California's Mount Shasta. These subterranean folk knew the secret of the mile-tall "disharmonic giants" who enslaved humankind during the "second cycle" of existence. Dr. Doreal was chosen as the Atlanteans messenger, channeling the word through Tibetan spirituality cross-pollinated with Biblical scripture. Doreal also drew heavily from his 30,000-volume collection of science fiction dime novels to fill in around the edges.

Sound crazy? Not to the 200 or so people who eventually followed him up to this isolated mountain community in the 1950s to escape the impending wrath of the Lemurians. Who are the Lemurians? The race of people living beneath the earth's surface, of course! They're prevented from exiting by the Atlanteans . . . at least until the atom bombs start dropping.

Dr. Doreal died in 1963, but his original temple still stands with a current following of about 100. You can see the outside from the road, but you can't enter unless you're a member. Reportedly, the temple has pews covered in padded blue leather, Tibetan temple bells, indirect aqua-colored lighting, and the former throne of Emperor Maximilian of Mexico sitting on a furry-white pedestal. Calling Hugh Hefner.

Jackson Creek Rd., Sedalia, CO 80135

Private phone

Hours: Always visible; view from road

Cost: Free

www.bwtemple.org

Directions: Drive south on Rte. 105 from Sedalia six miles, turn right on Jackson Creek Rd., and drive four miles west until you see the Temple on the right.

TRINIDAD

By law, you cannot play basketball before lunch in Trinidad.

Reason to protest.

Severance
Nuts!

Colorado is about as far from any ocean as you can get in the United States, which is why it seems strange that a roadside bar in this dinky plains community is known far and wide for its oysters. Rocky Mountain oysters, actually, and boy are they gooooood! They're only prepared one way—battered and deep-fried—the same way they've been serving them since 1957. And you won't get any fancy-schmancy Los Angeles oyster bar attitude in Severance either, no sirree. However, there does seem to be an informal dress code: camouflage coats, hunting caps, and hip waders.

The truth is, Rocky Mountain oysters don't come from the sea but from the scrotums of slaughtered bulls. Rancher types generally leave that little detail out when encouraging the city folk to try their Colorado delicacy. Testicles or not, they're mighty tasty, and nobody does them better than Bruce's, "where the geese fly and the bulls cry." Hey, is this why they call the town Severance?

Bruce's Bar, 345 First St., PO Box 114, Severance, CO 80546

(970) 686-2320

Hours: Sunday 10 A.M.–Midnight, Monday–Thursday 10 A.M.–10 P.M., Friday–Saturday 10 A.M.–2 A.M.

Cost: $7 All-You-Can-Eat Special

Directions: Just north of Rt. 68 on 23 Rd. (First St.).

Strasburg
The Real Golden Spike

When Leland Stanford drove the Golden Spike at Promontory Point, Utah, on May 10, 1869, he marked a dubious achievement: connecting Omaha, Nebraska, to Sacramento, California. Big deal. What thrill do you get from leaving Omaha if you end up in Sacramento, and vice versa?

Ah, but another railroad milestone 15 months later in Strasburg—now that was an accomplishment! When the Kansas Pacific Railroad joined its tracks three miles west of town at 3 P.M. on August 15, 1870, it completed the first continuous rail route from New York to San Francisco. Unlike the sham ceremony in Utah, this was the completion of the first true transcontinental railroad.

Comanche Crossing Museum, 56060 E. Colfax Ave., PO Box 647, Strasburg, CO 80136
(303) 622-4690

Hours: May–August, daily 1–4 P.M.

Cost: Free

Directions: Historic marker at the I-70 rest stop three miles west of Strasburg; Museum at the west end of town on Rte. 36 (Colfax Ave.).

ONE OF OUR LOCOMOTIVES IS MISSING!

Less than eight years after the Kansas Pacific Railroad completed its coast-to-coast marvel, it accomplished something even more amazing near the site of the original meeting place: it lost a locomotive. Forty tons of steel—it was nowhere to be found! Gone. Vanished.

Authorities knew it was last spotted between Strasburg and Bennett. On May 21, 1878, the eastbound KP freight train #8 plunged off a washed-out trestle into swollen Kiowa Creek, killing its two engineers and one rider. The locomotive sank in quicksand on the riverbed and was never recovered. Then, in 1979, author Clive Cussler tried to locate the train's remains in the dry creek bed . . . without any luck.

Sterling
The Living Trees

In most towns, city work crews remove dead and diseased trees, but that's not the case in Sterling. In this plains burg, they call Brad Rhea. Though he is not able to revive a dead tree in a biological sense, he can bring it back to life. Armed with a chisel and mallet, he uncovers a form deep within the wood: a mermaid, a golfer, a clown, a minuteman, a lion, or a group of giraffes.

Because trees die all over town, this is where you find Rhea's works, still attached to their roots. Here's a partial listing:

- *Stargrazers* (*Giraffes*), Columbine Park, Rte. 6 and 3rd Ave.
- *Father Time*, 702 Jackson St.
- *Seraphim*, Sterling Public Library, 425 N. 5th St.
- *Windlace*, Sterling Public Library, 425 N. 5th St.
- *Golfer*, Sterling Country Club, 17408 Highway 14
- *Plainsman Pete*, Monahan Library, NJC Campus, 100 College Dr.
- *Mask*, Dorothy Corsberg Theater, NJC Campus, 100 College Dr.
- *Burger King*, Burger King, 1027 W. Main St.

Unfortunately, bugs and elements take their toll on the dead trees, and some of Rhea's early work rotted. The *Stargrazers* have been replaced with a bronze casting.

Contact: Logan County Chamber of Commerce, 109 N. Front St., Sterling, CO 80751

(800) 544-8609 or (970) 522-5070 x598

E-mail: logancc@logancountychamber.com

Hours: Always visible

Cost: Free

www.logancountychamber.com/tourism/default.htm

Directions: All over town.

TRINIDAD

More sex reassignment surgeries are performed in Trinidad than in any other town in the nation.

France is nice, but it's not heaven.

Trinidad
Ave Maria Shrine

Miracles just ain't what they used to be. In 1908, Dr. John Espy spotted something glowing on a hillside just outside of Trinidad. Despite a blizzard, he made his way toward the light, which turned out to be a glowing statue of the Virgin Mary. Nobody could say how it got there. "A sign from God!" the locals shouted, and began digging into their pockets to build a shrine around the statue.

It was 1961 before the shrine was complete. Then, in 1962, somebody pushed the Virgin Mary over and her arms broke off. Inside her body were papers saying that she had been constructed in France, not sent from Heaven. Bummer. Nevertheless, the Virgin was repaired and locked up to discourage further vandalism. The shrine is still open, but it has lost some of its mystical aura.

Benedicta Ave., Trinidad, CO 81082

No phone

Hours: Daily 9 A.M.–6 P.M.

Cost: Free

Directions: At the east end of town; turn south on Benedicta Ave. from Rte. 160, head up the hill behind the hospital; follow the signs.

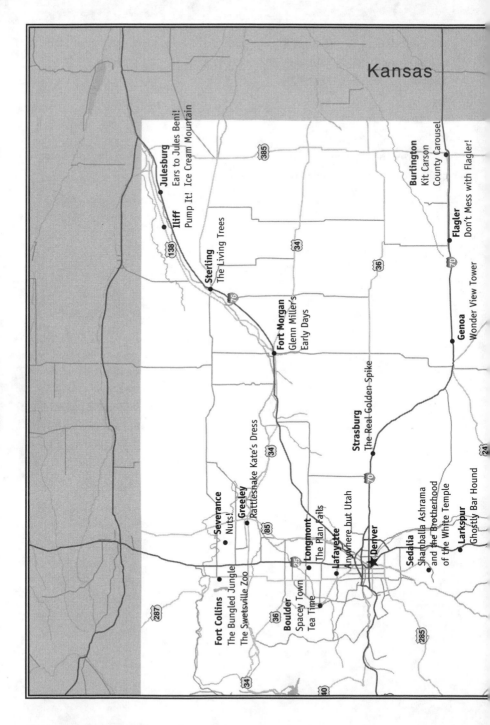

Kansas

Julesburg Ears to Jules Beni!
Iliff Pump It! Ice Cream Mountain

Burlington Kit Carson County Carousel

Flagler Don't Mess with Flagler!

Sterling The Living Trees

Fort Morgan Glenn Miller's Early Days

Genoa Wonder View Tower

Strasburg The Real Golden Spike

Severance Nuts!

Greeley Rattlesnake Kate's Dress

Longmont The Plan Falls

Lafayette Anywhere but Utah

Denver

Sedalia Shamballa Ashrama and the Brotherhood of the White Temple

Larkspur Ghostly Bar Hound

Fort Collins The Bungled Jungle The Swetsville Zoo

Boulder Spacey Town Tea Time

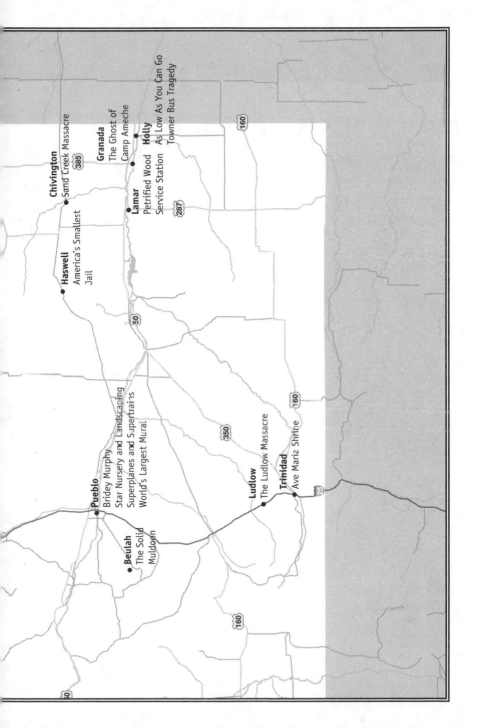

COLORADO SPRINGS AREA

$\mathcal{S}$omething sad is happening to Colorado Springs. The town's early economy was based on a rapid influx of tuberculosis patients who came west for the dry, thin air. (Estimates say 60 percent of the town's population had TB around the turn of the century.) These sick folk needed to be entertained, and one tourist trap spawned another: Pikes Peak, Cave of the Winds, Garden of the Gods, Seven Falls, and so on . . .

But rising property values and decreased interest in hokey entertainment have been eliminating the best the area has to offer. The Miracle House, a topsy-turvy house in East Manitou Springs, tried to appeal to 1950s hip cats: "Hey man, dig this crazy place!" and "Yeah, man, it's really *gone*! Like, way out!" It didn't work. The area's two wax museums have had meltdowns: the Hall of the Presidents Living Wax Studio had all the nation's chief executives, plus fairy-tale characters, astronauts, and Alferd Packer chowing down on his victims. The Buffalo Bill Wax Museum in Manitou Springs was filled with gunslingers.

Manitou Springs, much stranger (per capita) than its larger neighbor to the east, is morphing into one of those quaint mountain burgs where every other building is a cozy bed-and-breakfast or a wind-chime store. Yuck. Thankfully, the chamber of commerce hosts the Emma Crawford Coffin Races each October. The celebration commemorates a 1924 rainstorm that washed Crawford's casket and skeleton down from Red Mountain. Manitoids also hold a post-holiday Fruitcake Toss each January. Alas, it's an uphill battle against the "good taste" crowd. You'd better see these sites before Colorado Springs is no fun at all.

Colorado Springs
"A Cage for Birds"

Opened in 1958, the United States Air Force Academy looks like a boxy chicken coop (with a very nice chapel), or at least that's the way Frank Lloyd Wright saw it. His bid to design the new military academy was turned down in favor of a proposal from the architectural firm of Skidmore, Owings, and Merrill, so it might have been sour grapes when he called the campus "a cage for birds" and "a factory for birdmen."

Actually, that was the basic idea. Most of the academy's classrooms are windowless, which discourages daydreaming; they contain short-seated desks, which encourages stiff, upright (perched) posture. The only exception to this humorless campus are the uniforms designed by Hollywood director Cecil B. DeMille, which the Pentagon described as "attractive yet thoroughly masculine."

Barry Goldwater USAFA Visitor Center, 2346 Academy Dr., Colorado Springs, CO 80840

(719) 333-9400 or (719) 333-2025

Hours: June–August, daily 9 A.M.–6 P.M.; September–May, daily 9 A.M.–5 P.M.

Cost: Free

www.usafa.af.mil

Directions: Four miles west of the North Entrance (Exit 156) from I-25.

Colorado's 31st Highest Mountain

A few myths ought to be dispelled. Though it looks impressive, Pikes Peak doesn't even make the list of the top 30 tallest mountains in Colorado, let alone the United States. At 14,110 feet, it is surpassed by such lesser-known hills as Mount Democrat, Quandary Peak, and Mount Sneffels. It was originally named James Peak after Dr. Edwin James who, on July 14, 1820, was the first (documented) person to climb to its summit. During his 1806 journey west, Zebulon Pike never got any closer to his eventual namesake than 15 miles, nor did any member of his expedition. In fact, he logged the mountain in his journal as "unclimbable."

Pikes Peak has been the location of many famous events throughout the years. Over the course of 20 days in 1929, Bill Williams pushed a peanut to the top of the mountain . . . with his nose! Governor Teller Ammons lost the mountain in a 1938 football bet to the governor of Texas, but won it back before the Texans could have it moved south. And then there's the story of Katherine Lee Bates who rode to the top in a prairie wagon on July 22, 1893, and was inspired to write a poem she called "America the Beautiful." It was set to the music of "O Mother Dear, Jerusalem" by New Jersey organist Samuel A. Ward in 1895. For her effort, Bates received $5. Ward got nothing.

Every year on July 4, the mountain hosts the Pikes Peak Hill Climb. The auto race, first run in 1916, is the nation's second oldest, ranking right behind the Indy 500. Drivers maneuver the final 12.5 miles of the highway to the top. Ron Millen holds the record for the fastest climb in 1994: 10 minutes, 4.06 seconds. Whatever you do, *do not attempt to break the record*! If golf is more your speed, perhaps you'd enjoy the annual Pikes Peak Classic. Players tee off from the summit to a hole 6,000 feet below. Par is 24 strokes, and that's downhill.

There are several ways to get to the summit of Pikes Peak today. You can hike it—as the AdAmAn Club has been doing every December 31 since 1922—to shoot off fireworks. If you don't own a Yugo, you can drive 18.8 miles up the Toll Road, which opened in 1915. Easier still is the 1891 Cog Railway that leaves from Manitou Springs and chugs up the mountain on 46,158 feet of track. Once you reach the top, be sure to try the Summit House's famous High-Altitude Donuts. What makes them so airy? Water boils at 184°F up there.

PO Box 1575, M/C 060, Colorado Springs, CO 80901

(800) 318-9505 or (719) 385-PEAK

Hours: May–September, daily 7 A.M.–7 P.M.; October–April, daily 9 A.M.–3 P.M.

Cost: $10/person or $35/car, whatever's cheaper

www.pikespeakcolorado.com or www.pikespeakobservatory.com

Directions: Ten miles west of I-25 on Rte. 25, turn left on the Pikes Peak Toll Road at Cascade.

Cog Railway, 515 Ruxton Ave., PO Box 351, Manitou Springs, CO 80829

(719) 685-5401

E-mail: info@cograilway.com

Hours: April–October, call for departure times

Cost: July–August (high season), Adults $26.50, Kids (3–11) $14; (off season), Adults $25.50, Kids (3–11) $13.50

www.cograilway.com

Directions: Take Manitou Ave. to Ruxton, turn south, and head up the hill.

Dead Man's Canyon

More than a dozen people have reported seeing the ghost of William Harkens along Little Fountain Creek, which runs through the canyon named for this very unlucky, very dead settler. Harkens was murdered here by two Mexican religious zealots, Felipe and Julian Espinosa, on March 19, 1863.

Years earlier, in 1846, Felipe Espinosa had been orphaned when the U.S. Navy bombarded Vera Cruz, Mexico, killing his parents, his grandparents, and two of his siblings. Felipe claimed the Virgin Mary appeared to him in a dream with instructions to kill 100 Americans for every family member that had perished. Do the math: Mary asked him to off 600 gringos. It was a big task, so he enlisted the help of his cousin Julian.

Harkens, the pair's third victim, was found with an ax stuck in his skull. Friends laid him to rest, but he apparently hasn't found much peace. Those who've spotted his angry spirit claim he tries to run off anyone who disturbs the site of his old cabin. You'll know if it's him if you see a guy with an ax in his head. That is, if he's moving.

And what happened to the Espinosas? After terrifying Anglo settlers throughout the state, and butchering 26 of them, the pair were tracked down and killed by Tom Tobin. The mountainman brought their heads to the territorial governor for the $1,500 bounty, but the politician never paid out. The noggins were rediscovered years later in a tunnel under the state capitol.

Route 115, Colorado Springs, CO 80926

No phone

Hours: Best after dark

Cost: Free

Directions: Ten miles south of town on Rte. 115, toward Cañon City.

COLORADO SPRINGS
Lon Chaney was born in Colorado Springs on April 1, 1883. His first name was Alonzo. Chaney lived in Colorado Springs until he was 19.

Pleeeeeease keep to the right!

Garden of the Gods

Back when this region was settled, Colorado City founders Colonel Melancthon Beach and Rufus Cable came across red sandstone formations northwest of present-day Colorado Springs. Colonel Beach suggested that the area would make a great beer garden. The pious Cable disagreed, "Beer garden indeed! Why, this is a place for the gods to assemble!" Cable won out in the end, and the 770-acre park was proclaimed the Garden of the Gods.

Assigning names to the stunning red spires has proved to be a task akin to cloud gazing; sometimes you can see what the titles describe; more often it's a stretch. Kissing Camels, Siamese Twins, Tower of Babel, Toad and Toadstools, Baldheaded Scotchman, Punch and Judy, and Balanced Rock are fairly obvious, while Giant Sandals, Pig's Eye, Steamboat Rock, Baby Elephant, Irish Washerwoman, and Egyptian Mummy are

tough. Seal and Bear was once known as Seal Making Love to a Nun, but it was changed because of complaints, and the man who named it was fired. However, you can still make out that frisky critter if you look at it just right. Similarly, objections from some religious folk over the years have resulted in names like Montezuma Temple Ruins being changed to Cathedral Spires; the Three Graces from Greek mythology—Brightness, Joy, and Bloom—have been given monotheistic references: Faith, Hope, and Love. Oddly, Devil's Pulpit remains, as does Baked Potato.

No trip to the Garden of the Gods would be complete without a visit to the Trading Post, a Pueblo-style knickknack shop opened in 1901. It's got everything from high-end Native American art to 1950s buckaroo kitsch. There's also a snack shop.

But you know what this area could *really* use? A beer garden.

Garden of the Gods Visitor's Center, 1805 N. 30th St., Colorado Springs, CO 80904
(719) 634-6666
Hours: Daily 5 A.M.–11 P.M.
Cost: Free
www.gardenofthegods.com
Directions: Exit 146 from I-25, head west to 30th St., turn south to Gateway Rd.

Garden of the Gods Trading Post, 324 Beckers Lane, Manitou Springs, CO 80829
(800) 874-4515 or (719) 685-9045
Hours: June–August, daily 5 A.M.–8 P.M.; September–May, daily 9 A.M.–5:30 P.M.
Cost: Free
www.co-trading-post.com
Directions: Take Manitou Ave. east from Rte. 24, turn north on Beckers Lane.

Ghost Town Museum

The trouble with so many Colorado ghost towns is that they're often in the middle of nowhere, hard to reach without four-wheel drive, and falling apart.

Not so with Pikes Peak Ghost Town, located on the southwest side of Colorado Springs. The owners have crammed the remnants of an entire mining town into two buildings, including a jail, blacksmith, saloon, general store, barbershop, and more. Watch out for the smooth-talking dummy in the jail; he'll make you an offer to split his cache of stolen gold if you spring him from the pokey! Step into the saloon and check out nickelodeon flip-movies such as "Naughty, Naughty Boss" whose sexual harassment of a job applicant leads to cat fight between the poor woman and the boss's jealous assistant—*meow*! There's more old-time high jinks to be had at the boarding house where a bosomy mannequin waves a hanky at you from her red-lit room. You can look all you want, but there are no stairs to her second-floor bordello.

One sad thing about Pikes Peak Ghost Town's large collection of artifacts is what you *don't* see on display. Somewhere, tucked away in a warehouse, are treasures from America's attic: Eleanor Roosevelt's ice skates, FDR's 1942 bulletproof Lincoln limousine, and the buggy Chester A. Arthur rode to his inauguration. Apparently some historical nitpicker pointed out that these don't really belong in a western ghost town. Boo!

600 S. 21st St., Colorado Springs, CO 80904

(719) 634-0696

E-mail: history@ghosttownmuseum.com

Hours: May–October, Monday–Saturday 9 A.M.–6 P.M., Sunday 1–6 P.M.;
   November–April, Saturday–Sunday 1–4 P.M.

Cost: Adults $5, Seniors $4.50, Kids $2.50

www.ghosttownmuseum.com

Directions: Just south of Rte. 24 on 21st St., behind Van Briggle Art Pottery.

Kempf's Kreations

Geez, try to add a little class to a neighborhood and what do you get? Grief—that's what! Architect and artist Starr Gideon Kempf and his wife Hedwig moved to Cheyenne Canyon in 1948, and everything was hunky-dory until Starr erected his first wind sculpture in 1978. By then, the couple's once-remote home was surrounded by other, less interesting houses. Kempf created 10 graceful steel artworks, some as tall as 50 feet, and placed them on his front lawn. Two of the largest pieces are birds, one in flight and the other apparently trying to lay an egg. There's also a "Space Needle" and an elaborate sun, and they all spin smoothly with the breezes blowing out of the canyon.

They are not noisy. They are not ugly. But they attract tourists—too many, according to the neighbors.

Did the Kempfs complain when the neighbors built homes nearby and started cluttering up the view? No. So why are the locals upset?

Obnoxious visitors, tour buses that leave their engines running, Winnebagos that unsuccessfully turn around in their driveways and flatten the hedges, and the catch-all complaint: property values. According to them, this public art makes their ho-hum, million-dollar homes worth less. Whatever. When you stop by for a visit to Kempf's Kreations (and you should!), remember: don't be a jerk—this is a residential street.

2057 Pine Grove Ave., Colorado Springs, CO 80906

Private phone

Hours: Always visible

Cost: Free

Directions: One block south of Cheyenne Blvd. at South Cheyenne Creek.

FUN TIMES AT COLORADO SPRINGS' HIGH SCHOOLS

Few graduates of the Colorado Springs school system have made as big an impression as **Cassandra Peterson**. A member of the class of 1969 at Palmer High School (301 N. Nevada Ave.), Peterson is best known by her stage name: Elvira, Mistress of the Dark.

Another woman of mystery, **Cheyen Weatherly**, enrolled at Coronado High School (1590 W. Filmore Street) in the fall of 1990. A standout on the cheerleading squad, she was able to perform all the lifts needed for the most physically demanding pep formations. Several members of the Coronado football team were trying to date her when staff discovered she was not a Greek exchange student, but Charles Daugherty, a 26-year-old drag queen with a rap sheet that included theft, burglary, and check fraud. What's even more amazing, Daugherty had pulled the same stunt a year earlier by getting a spot on the Colorado Springs Spirit football cheerleading team, this time masquerading as Shannon Trump, fictitious niece of billionaire Donald Trump.

Though he did not attend high school here, **John Cameron Mitchell** spent some of his post-teen life in Colorado Springs, the son of an army major general. Mitchell's alter ego, Hedwig, is the star of *Hedwig and the Angry Inch*, a stage show (and later movie) about a German transsexual dealing with the aftereffects of a botched sex-change operation.

Where's Mothra when you need her?

May's Natural History Museum of the Tropics, World's Largest Hercules Beetle, and Museum of Space Exploration

When you first see the Hercules beetle looming over the highway south of town, fear races through your mind. How has this insect grown to its enormous size? Has there been a mutant-creating nuclear accident?

Maybe it's part of some sinister government plot hatched deep within Cheyenne Mountain!

Fear not, traveler! Draw close and you'll notice that the 16-foot-long, 10-foot-high bug is surrounded by a storm fence, has no legs, and couldn't chase you even if it were alive. This Hercules beetle is just a sign to point the way to May's Natural History Museum of the Tropics. Three generations of the May family have collected tropical insects from all points on the globe, and now the bugs are back here, pinned to corkboard in glass cases. They're meticulously mounted and labeled, from the tiniest mites to dinner plate–sized tarantulas munching on dead hummingbirds. The museum has only enough room to display 7,000 of the 100,000 specimens in its collection, so for every bug you see, there are a dozen more somewhere. Do you suddenly feel itchy?

Your paid admission also gets you into the Museum of Space Exploration across the parking lot. Three trailer homes form a triangular structure filled with what appear to be science fair projects. Each exhibit is a crude plastic model glued to foam board with pages ripped from science magazines and NASA handouts glued around it.

710 Rock Creek Canyon Rd., Colorado Springs, CO 80926
(800) 666-3841 or (719) 576-0450
E-mail: maymuseum2001@yahoo.com
Hours: May–September, daily 9 A.M.–7 P.M.
Cost: Adults $4.50, Seniors (60+) $3.50, Kids (6–12) $2.50
www.maymuseum-camp-rvpark.com
Directions: Five miles south of town on Rte. 115; look for the beetle on the west side of the road, turn west on Rock Creek Canyon Rd., and follow the signs.

Money Museum

Numismatics is not what makes your joints ache when you get old, nor is it that math course you flunked in college. It's the general term used to describe coins, paper currency, medals, and other money-related items. The American Numismatics Association is headquartered in Colorado Springs, and this is their institutional collection.

This organization's impressive holdings are displayed on a rotating schedule. Some of their more popular exhibits include the Hall of Nations with jumbo 3D renderings of the world's coins, the Abraham

Lincoln Collection (no Confederate bills in this one!), a bartering selection, and the Hall of Presidents with coins and currency dating from the birth, inauguration, and death of each U.S. president. They've also got $3 bills, beaver-shaped tokens used in the Hudson Bay Company's stores, and stone currency from the Island of Yap. Best of all, you don't have to part with any of your own coins to see them—the museum's free!

Museum of the American Numismatic Association, 818 N. Cascade Ave., Colorado Springs, CO 80903

(800) 367-9723 or (719) 632-2646

E-mail: anamus@money.org

Hours: Monday–Friday 9 A.M.–4 P.M., Saturday 10 A.M.–4 P.M.

Cost: Free

www.money.org

Directions: Four blocks south of Uintah Ave., four blocks east of I-25.

Nikola Tesla Comes to Town

Croatian-born inventor Nikola Tesla came to Colorado Springs in May 1899 when his experiments had grown too large, loud, and lethal to conduct in his New York City lab. He set up a new research station a mile east of downtown near the Colorado School for the Deaf and Blind (good thing!). During his stay he lived at the Alta Vista Hotel in Room 207, a suite he found acceptable because it was divisible by the number 3. Only Tesla knew why this was important.

Funded primarily by millionaire John Jacob Astor, Tesla erected a 200-foot-tall Tesla generator on the wide-open Colorado prairie, powered via eight miles of coiling wire. His ultimate goal was to transmit a wireless message from Pikes Peak to the Paris Exposition of 1900, and expose frauds like Marconi and Edison.

When he fired it up at full throttle one summer evening in 1899, his tower shot 135-foot lightning-bolt sparks that could be heard crackling as far away as Cripple Creek—on the other side of Pikes Peak! Nearby horses ran wild from the noise and the electrical charges conducted through the soil to their metal shoes. But the show didn't last long; the generator overloaded the city's power plant, causing an explosion and fire. The entire city suffered a blackout. To avoid being run out of town on a rail, electric or otherwise, Tesla had his workers assist in the rebuilding efforts. Within a year, however, Tesla moved back east.

Though in some ways he fit the stereotype of a mad scientist, Tesla made many important discoveries. Tesla transmitted radio messages two years before Marconi, discovered X-ray prints which he called shadow graphs, and popularized alternating current. In 1892, much to the amusement of other scientists, he claimed that he received messages from other planets. Yet Tesla was partially correct; the messages had not been transmitted by little green aliens, but were instead background noise from space. Tesla also once tried to get the U.S. military interested in a death ray to knock airplanes out of the sky. Surprisingly, they didn't take him up on it.

The folks of Colorado Springs have not forgotten the nutty professor. The International Tesla Society is located in town, but its museum is currently closed. If you want to see its collection, you have to join the society. Another benefit of membership is getting discounts on all the kooky products, such as the Tesla Mosquito Terminal, engine-saving Space Oil, and "Rare Earth" Magnetizer Biomagnets.

Foote & Pikes Peak Aves., Colorado Springs, CO 80909

No phone

Hours: Always visible

Cost: Free

Directions: Lab was two blocks east of the Colorado School for the Deaf and Blind; four
   blocks west of Union Blvd. and four blocks south of Boulder St.

Contact: International Tesla Institute, PO Box 38335, Colorado Springs, CO 80937

(719) 632-4327

E-mail: teslapro@uswest.net

www.tesla.org/welcome.htm

NORAD

A remnant of the Cold War, the North American Air Defense Command (NORAD) spends less of its time today watching for Russian missiles than it does tracking satellites in orbit. Every time one is about to drop from the sky, NORAD is there to pinpoint when and where, at least within a thousand miles or so.

Opened in 1965, the 4.5-acre complex is buried 1,200 feet deep inside Cheyenne Mountain behind 30-ton, 25-foot-thick doors. It rests on springs to cushion it from a direct nuclear strike. How many civilians do you think they intended to let ride out an atomic attack should the need have arisen? Did you see *Dr. Strangelove?*

Some UFO experts claim the NORAD facility is also the final resting place for the aliens recovered from the Roswell incident. Could that be the reason you have to book your tour six months in advance, or why the taking of photographs is forbidden? Are they hiding little dead green men in their closets? Don't ask because they won't tell. What they *will* tell you is the incoming trajectory of Santa's sleigh on Christmas Eve— NORAD issues a live report on this critical phenomenon each year. Your tax dollars at work.

There has been some talk about retooling NORAD for homeland security in the wake of September 11, but nothing has been finalized yet. Don't hold your breath for public tours if the facility changes its mission.

Contact: Tour Program, 250 S. Peterson Blvd., Suite 116, Peterson AFB, CO 80914

(719) 474-2241

Hours: Book six months in advance

Cost: Free

www.spacecom.af.mil/norad/index.htm

Directions: You'll get them when they're ready to give them to you.

Pro Rodeo Hall of Fame and Museum of the American Cowboy

What kind of fool willingly jumps on the back of an angry bull or bucking bronco? Who would voluntarily wrestle a steer to the ground barehanded, or dress up like a clown to attract the attention of a pissed-off, 2,000-pound, still-kicking, raging pile of beef? An inductee at this museum, that's who! The folks at the Pro Rodeo Hall of Fame don't want you to look at them like they're a bunch of yahoos with death wishes; they're trained athletic professionals. Try all you want, gang, but you'd never get me on one of them thar thangs.

The Pro Rodeo Cowboys Association was formed in 1936 after Boston promoters tried to screw their rodeo's performers. The cowboys walked, and then they started their own organization. Today, members are honored at this unique museum. Here you'll find dozens of display cases with artifacts from famous steer wrestlers, calf ropers, bull riders, saddle broncs, barebacks, clowns, announcers, and All-Around Cowboys, too many of whom have been long since gored or trampled . . . many, many times.

Lest you think cowboys have no respect for the critters they ride, or attempt to ride, there's a special Hall of Fame category for animals: stock. Some stock have calm, misleading names such as Peanuts and Skoal Sippin' Velvet; but more names reflect their true nature: Come Apart, Tornado, and Hell's Angel.

101 Pro Rodeo Dr., Colorado Springs, CO 80919

(719) 528-4764

Hours: Daily 9 A.M.–5 P.M.

Cost: Adults $6, Seniors $5, Kids (6–12) $3

www.prorodeo.com

Directions: One block west of I-25 on Rockimmon Blvd. (Exit 147), at Pro Rodeo Dr.

Seven Falls

What a difference electricity makes! Before this natural wonder was upgraded, visitors could only appreciate this 181-foot, seven-step waterfall during the daytime, and then only if their hearts could withstand the grueling 224 steps to the summit.

Developers have since added multicolored lights so folks could see the cascade late into the evening. To make the falls more accessible to the cardiac-challenged, a Mountain Express Elevator was installed. Today, the only steps you have to worry about are the ones going *down*. But if you're interested in a hike, take the one-mile trail from the top of the falls to the grave of Helen Hunt Jackson. This settler wrote about the mistreatment Native Americans and the importance of nature. If she hadn't died in 1885, she might have had a thing or two to say about Seven Falls' mood lighting and the hiker helper.

2850 S. Cheyenne Canyon Rd., PO Box 118, Colorado Springs, CO 80901

(719) 632-0765

Hours: September–May, daily 9 A.M.–4:15 P.M.; June–August, daily 8:30 A.M.–10:30 P.M.

Cost (Day/Night): Adults $7/$8.50, Seniors $6/$6, Kids (6–15) $4.50/$5.50

www.sevenfalls.com

Directions: Follow the signs on S. Cheyenne Canyon Rd., west of the Broadmoor Hotel.

Turin Shroud Center of Colorado

Dirty tablecloth from the Last Supper? Burial shroud of the son of God? Fourteenth-century religious hoax? Some combination of the three? If anyone's going to figure it out, it's the staff at this place. Started in 1990, the Turin Shroud Center is this country's most active research institute devoted to the study of this mysterious holy relic. In addition to being an outlet for publications and videos, they've got an impressive collection of reproduced artifacts, but you can only see them if you're willing to take a course offered by one of their researchers.

Central to their collection is a high-definition, full-size photographic replica of the shroud hanging on a 14-foot lighted wall. The slide has been marked where key pieces of evidence have been found, like the blood splotches near the wound sites. You'll also see food and wine stains that might indicate it was first used as the tablecloth for the Farewell Din-Din. An anatomically correct Jesus model reclines in the middle of the center's study space, wrapped in a new linen shroud and sporting a crown of thorns.

Radiocarbon dating in 1988 suggested that the artifact held in Turin, Italy, is only 700 years old, but that conclusion has been challenged by Moscow scientist Dmitri Koutsentsov. A 1532 fire in Chambrey, France, damaged part of the cloth, and Koutsentsov claims it contaminated the shroud's fibers, making it impossible to determine its actual age. You'll get all the details if you take a course. Don't think you have to be a believer to participate in one of the classes, but be aware that these folks take this stuff *very* seriously. They expect you to at least give their research open-minded consideration.

PO Box 25326, Colorado Springs, CO 80918

(719) 599-5755 or (719) 599-9249

E-mail: tscience@rmi.net

Hours: By appointment

Cost: Depends on the program

www.shroudofturin.com

Directions: You will be given directions at the time you make an appointment.

COLORADO SPRINGS
America's first labor union, the International Typographical Union (ITU), was founded in Colorado Springs in 1852.

Uncle Wilbur Fountain

During the summer, Uncle Wilbur pops up every hour or so at a Colorado Springs park, tootling his horn while children dance around him in their bathing suits. And while this might make some parents nervous, there's no need to be alarmed—Uncle Wilbur is a *robot*!

In an effort to breathe a little life into a dying city park, the Smokebrush Foundation donated a kinetic water sculpture that is much more than a standard throw-a-coin-and-make-a-wish fountain. On the hour, a seemingly stationary blue half-sphere rises from its mosaic-encrusted pedestal as 150 water jets erupt onto any kids or adults standing too close. Uncle Wilbur has arrived! A spotted monkey dances around the old man, serenaded by a tuba tune. Though you may get a little wet, you will be encouraged to solve the riddle embedded in the tiles along the fountain's base. If you're not particularly good at riddles, you're likely to get a *lot* wet.

But who is the real Uncle Wilbur? you ask. None other than Wilbur Fulker, former principal of the Colorado School for the Deaf and Blind and uncle to Bob Tudor, one of the fountain's co-creators.

Acacia Park, 201 N. Tejon, Colorado Springs, CO 80903

(719) 444-1012

Hours: May–August, on the hour

Cost: Free

www.smokebrush.com

Directions: At the corner of Bijou and Tejon Aves. three blocks north of Colorado Ave.

World Figure Skating Museum and Hall of Fame

When you tour the World Figure Skating Museum and Hall of Fame, two thoughts will turn over and over in your mind: (1) these skaters are wee things, and (2) they sure do like silver bowls. If you were to remove every Barbie- or Ken-size costume, and every etched silver punch bowl, there would be little left here to look at. Oh, they've got skates and sculptures and Olympic medals, but they aren't half as recognizable as Scott Hamilton's red and blue jumpsuit from the 1984 Sarajevo games or Tara Lipinski's spangled one-piece number. You'll also see classic clothing from famous skaters you probably never did get to see, such as Dick Button's 1948 bellhop jacket, and the gown Sonja Henie wore to John F. Kennedy's inaugural ball.

One of the things you *won't* be seeing is the object that brought so much attention to this sport in recent years: the billy club swung by Tanya Harding's hitman in an attempt to break Nancy Kerrigan's knee. Deny it if you will, but that incident did more to bring a new audience to skating than any in recent history. Oddly, it made these graceful athletes seem a little more human.

20 First St., Colorado Springs, CO 80906

(719) 635-5200

Hours: June–August, Monday–Saturday 10 A.M.–4 P.M.; September–May, Monday–
   Friday, 1st Saturdays 10 A.M.–4 P.M.

Cost: Adults $3, Kids (6–12) $2

www.worldskatingmuseum.org or www.usfsa.org

Directions: One block north of the Broadmoor Hotel, where First St. meets Lake Ave.

World's Crookedest Highway

If you take a trip up the Broadmoor–Cheyenne Highway out of Colorado Springs and you feel like you're going nowhere, you're right! Though the road is seven miles long, it's all been compacted into 1.5 square miles of mountainside. In other words, it's the World's Crookedest Highway.

The road passes several landmarks as it twists its way up Cheyenne Mountain. The first, the Cheyenne Mountain Zoo (4250 Cheyenne Mountain Zoo Rd., www.cmzoo.org) is the only U.S. zoo located on a mountain. Just above the zoo is the Will Rogers Shrine of the Sun. Builder Spencer Penrose had intended for Rogers to be entombed here after he died, but the humorist's family had other plans. After he perished in an Alaska plane crash, his body was returned to his birthplace in Oklahoma for burial. The nerve!

Broadmoor–Cheyenne Highway, Colorado Springs, CO 80906

No phone

Hours: Always open, weather permitting

Cost: Free

Directions: Follow the signs to the zoo from the Broadmoor.

FORT CARSON
Clark Gable was stationed at Fort Carson during World War II.

All the fun with none of the frostbite.
Photo by author, courtesy of the North Pole/Santa's Workshop

Suburbs
Cascade
North Pole/Santa's Workshop

No, you're not imagining things—the North Pole is in Colorado! Don't worry, the earth hasn't shifted on its axis since you last checked. The

North Pole is a Christmas-themed amusement park designed in 1956 by a former artist at Walt Disney. Though it is not geographically accurate, it sure *looks* authentic with dozens of kiddie rides decorated with candy canes, icicles, and ornaments, each run by a gangly teenager in an elf costume.

The carnival rides are just half the fun. Stop into Miss Muffet's Snacks for a bite to eat—but don't worry about spiders that might sit down beside you. Visit the teepee-shaped Indian Gift Shop to pick up western curios such as rubber tomahawks and Davy Crockett caps made from rabbit hides. And if you've been a good boy or girl, pay Santa a visit and give him your wish list for next year. Boy, if this place were any more 1950s, you'd be on the set of *Leave It to Beaver*.

The North Pole is an efficient operation; every time you make a purchase inside the park, an elf delivers your merchandise to the front gate. You pick up your goodies on the way out. Whether the jolly atmosphere has a calming effect is unclear, but the clientele do seem less pushy than at the average amusement park. Then again, that might be the altitude.

When you enter, pay special attention to the many rules posted at the park gate. A favorite: "Anyone annoying to other guests can be ejected without a refund." Maybe that's why the elves don't sing.

Pikes Peak Highway & Rte. 24, Cascade, CO 80809

(719) 684-9432

E-mail: santashelper@santas-colo.com

Hours: May, Friday–Tuesday 10 A.M.–5 P.M.; June–August, daily 9:30 A.M.–6 P.M.;
September–December, Friday–Tuesday 10 A.M.–5 P.M.

Cost: Adults $12.95, Seniors (60+) $5.50, Kids (2+) $12.95

www.santas-colo.com

Directions: Ten miles west of I-25 on Rte. 24, turn left on the Pikes Peak Toll Road and
follow the signs.

GREEN MOUNTAIN FALLS

Bigfoot has been spotted several times in Green Mountain Falls since 1980. In 1988, several blond-haired Bigfeet trashed a cabin near town.

Manitou Springs
Cave of the Winds

Cave of the Winds is one of those unapologetic kitschy pull-offs from a bygone era of bad taste. While some American caverns have succumbed to the pressure to be educational, this place still offers healthy doses of hokum.

You know you're at a tourist trap when, "for security purposes," they insist on snapping a photo of every guest against a stalactite backdrop before the tour begins. As you pass through the cave's 20 rooms, your guide points out descriptions of formations such as E.T. Sinking in the Mud, and bombards you with corny jokes. "The formations hanging down are called stalactites. The formations rising from the floor are called stalagmites. And these," your guide will tell you, pointing to the recessed electrical fixtures, "are *stalaglights*." At the end of the tour this joker tries to sell you the security photo as a souvenir.

Cave of the Winds was discovered by a group of kids on a Sunday school outing in 1880. The kids followed the low hum of the winds blowing over the entrance in Williams Canyon. On February 15, 1881, it opened for its first tours. Over the years, the site has been improved and the caverns have been expanded—you no longer have to enter on your hands and knees carrying a candle. In the summer, in addition to your cave tour, you're invited to watch the Laser Canyon Show from the bleachers overlooking the entrance hut cliff.

Serpentine Dr., PO Box 826, Manitou Springs, CO 80829

(719) 685-5444

E-mail: info@caveofthewinds.com

Hours: June–August, daily 9 A.M.–9 P.M.; September–April, 10 A.M.–5 P.M.

Laser Canyon Shows: May, Friday–Saturday 9 P.M.; June–August, daily 9 P.M.

Cost: Discovery Tour, Adults $15, Kids (6–15) $8; Lantern Tour, Adults $18, Kids (6–15) $9; Explorer Tour (13+) $80, No Kids

www.caveofthewinds.com

Directions: Six miles west of I-25 off Rte. 24, follow the signs; on the north side of the highway.

MANITOU SPRINGS

A UFO was spotted "dancing" in the skies over Manitou Springs on May 19, 1947.

It's a better fit if you're a little green man.

Funky Arcades

Do you miss Skee Ball, Pac Man, or Bally's Playboy Pinball? Do you long to test your amorous prowess with an electric Love Machine, swat ball bearings with a tiny mechanical bat, or ride in a kiddie space capsule? Then look no farther than downtown Manitou Springs where a half-dozen amusement arcades are trapped in time. While arcades across the nation have chucked their Space Invaders consoles to make way for virtual reality Indy racers at $2 a pop, it's nice to find a place where you can still be entertained with the change in your pockets.

Straddling the creek in the center of town, the funky arcades of Manitou Springs look like a burial ground for electronic amusements machines. Most still work; some date back to the 1920s. They seem to have been thrown together the same way they fell off the delivery truck, so if you're looking for a childhood favorite, it might take some time. But that's half the fun; in the quest for Pong, you'll get your palm read, battle Elton John with rubber flippers, and torpedo German U-boats. What better place to get in touch with your inner nerd?

Family Fun Arcade Amusements, Inc., Manitou & Navajo Aves., Manitou Springs, CO 80829

(719) 685-9815

Hours: Sunday–Thursday, 11 A.M.–8 P.M., Friday–Saturday 11 A.M.–9 P.M.

Cost: 1¢, 5¢, 10¢, and 25¢

Directions: On Manitou Ave. at Navajo Ave., in the center of town.

Manitou Cliff Dwellings Museum

Why spend a whole day driving down to the southwest corner of the state to see a bunch of dilapidated Indian ruins, especially if you can see them on the Front Range, within biking distance of Colorado Springs?

Sure, they're not entirely authentic—the Anasazi never lived on Pikes Peak. The dwellings were relocated here from faraway McElmo Canyon in 1906, and they are in a lot better shape than most of the originals out in the desert. And because the 40-room tour is self-guided, you won't have a grumpy, overworked park ranger telling you to watch your step and keep your hands off the artifacts.

Route 24 Bypass, PO Box 272, Manitou Springs, CO 80829

(800) 354-9971 or (719) 685-5242

E-mail: info@cliffdwellingsmuseum.com

Hours: November–April, daily 9 A.M.–5 P.M.; May & September, daily 9 A.M.–6 P.M.; June–August, daily 9 A.M.–8 P.M.

Cost: Adults $8, Seniors (60+) $7, Kids (7–11) $6, Seniors (100+) Free

www.cliffdwellingsmuseum.com

Directions: North of town off the Rte. 24 Bypass.

Woodland Park
Capture of the Texas 7

Here's some advice: if a bunch of young toughs with dyed hair arrive at your trailer park and tell you they're simple Christians looking to "commune with nature" in the dead of winter, don't believe them. Especially if they spend their afternoons hiding in their RV with the music blaring, coming out mostly at night to shoot pool at a local tavern. That's what happened after seven guys showed up at the Coachlight Trailer Park on January 1, 2001.

They turned out to be heavily armed fugitives who'd escaped from a Kenedy, Texas, facility on December 13. While fleeing to Colorado, they killed policeman Aubrey Hawkins on Christmas Eve outside Oshman's Sporting Goods in Irving, Texas. Only after they were featured on *America's Most Wanted* was somebody able to identify these criminals hiding in Woodland Park.

The FBI nabbed George Rivas, Michael Rodriguez, and Joseph Garcia when they stopped at the Western Gas and Convenience Shop (20421 W. U.S. Highway 24, Woodland Park) on January 22. Meanwhile, agents surrounded the gang's RV back at the Coachlight, where Larry Harper shot himself before he was captured. Thirty-five loaded guns were discovered inside.

The two remaining fugitives, Patrick Murphy and Donald Newbury, ditched a van they'd been using behind the Hungry Farmer Restaurant (575 Garden of the Gods Road, Colorado Springs), then hightailed it over to a nearby Holiday Inn. Acting on another tip, police surrounded the hotel on January 24. Before being taken into custody, the pair talked with a reporter from KKTV to air their grievances, among them, "[t]here is a definite wrong within the penal system of the state of Texas." No kidding. Number 1 problem: they let their criminals escape.

After being captured, the cons became celebrities at what had been their favorite hangout while on the lam: the Tres Hombres Tex-Mex Cantina (116.5 W. Midland Avenue, Woodland Park) where shameless profiteers sold $20 "Texas 7" T-shirts to any dumb sucker who wanted to commemorate the bloody events.

Coachlight Motel and Trailer Park, 19253 E. U.S. Highway 24, Woodland Park, CO 80863 (719) 687-8732

Hours: Always visible

Cost: Free

Directions: Just south of Aspen Garden Way on Rte. 24.

Holiday Inn, Room 426, 505 Popes Bluff Tr., Colorado Springs, CO 80907

(800) 962-5470

Hours: Always visible

Cost: Free

Directions: Just north and west of the Garden of the Gods exit from I-25.

4

THE MOUNTAINS

To hear Coloradoans brag about their mountains, you'd think they'd pushed them up themselves. Sure, the Rockies are stunning, but they were beautiful long before humans ever set foot in the region. If you've surveyed the view of the Climax molybdenum mine from atop Fremont Pass, you know that some places looked better before anyone showed up. But what, if anything, have local folks done to *improve* these pristine peaks?

As it turns out, a lot! Who started a unique colony of alligators in a mountain hot spring? Humans. What about the Ice Palace that once soared over Leadville, America's Highest City—who made that? Yep, humans. And who erected the world's highest suspension bridge, who molded a 42-foot, concrete, hot dog–shaped fast-food joint, and who carved a firehouse into a solid rock cliff? Humans, humans, and more humans.

Please understand, I'm not badmouthing Mother Nature—she's done a fine job. But who speaks for the drive-in movie motels, the jumbo rocking chairs, the UFO observation towers, and the haunted pioneer graveyards in Colorado's high country? Who will tell you the full stories behind Alferd Packer, the state's favorite cannibal; the Old Homestead, Colorado's only brothel museum; and Prunes and Shorty, two big asses that Fairplay residents took into their hearts? I will, and I'm a human.

Alamosa
Snippy Snipped to Pieces

Black helicopters. Satanic cults. Cattle mutilations. They're all part of America's mysterious modern folklore, and almost all can be traced back to the story of Snippy the Horse.

The tale goes something like this. A three-year-old Appaloosa owned by Nellie Lewis was found dead on the King Ranch, just south of the Great Sand Dunes, on September 7, 1967. Snippy was not in good shape. The skin on his head and neck had been completely removed and his skull was bleached white. His internal organs were missing, including his brain, yet the remainder of his body was intact. Stranger still, Snippy's hoofprints ended 100 yards from where his body came to rest, and several dark, conical holes were found some distance from the carcass. Alien abduction? Cult sacrifice? Both?

The facts of the case suggest otherwise. First of all, the oft-repeated account above is riddled with inaccuracies. The horse in question was named Lady, not Snippy. Snippy sired Lady, but reporters felt "Snippy" fit the news stories better, and it stuck. Although it is seldom reported, the so-called Snippy's body contained two bullets, likely fired from a non-Martian rifle. And why do original reports of an earthbound purple pup tent sighted near the horse's body on the day of the mutilation—as opposed to, say, a flying saucer—never make their way into the ever-weirder story?

Nellie Lewis apparently started the speculation that a UFO was involved, and in the years following the horse's death she descended into her own private mental hell. Lewis claimed she was hounded wherever she went by flying saucers, which constantly banged their metal hulls on the roofs of buildings where she stayed. Lewis killed herself at an Alamosa cemetery in March 1976 by running a hose from the tail pipe into her car.

After rotting several months on the San Luis Valley floor, what was left of Snippy was taken to Alamosa. The bones were mounted and placed in the window of a pottery shop on Route 285, and later donated to the Luther Bean Museum at Adams State (Richardson Hall, Room 256). Then, sometime in the last decade, Snippy disappeared! Were Martians involved? Better call Scully and Mulder!

Harry King Ranch, Rte. 150, Alamosa, CO 81101

No phone

Hours: Always visible

Cost: Free

Directions: Three miles south of Great Sand Dunes National Monument on Sand Dunes Rd. (Rte 150).

Aspen
Ted Bundy's First Colorado Escape

Ted Bundy left a trail of victims across the west in the early 1970s, and Colorado had its share. On January 12, 1975, Caryn Campbell disappeared from Room 210 of **Aspen**'s Wildwood Inn while vacationing with her fiancé and his two children. Her body was found several miles away along Owl Creek on February 18. Julie Cunningham vanished in **Vail** on March 15 and was never found. Denise Oliverson was riding her bike in **Grand Junction** when she was abducted on April 6; her bike and sandals were found under a railroad bridge on Route 50; her body never was. Melanie Cooley was last seen hitchhiking from high school in **Nederland** on April 15. Her body turned up in Coal Creek Canyon on April 23. Shelley Robertson of **Golden** disappeared on July 1; she was found dead inside a mine on Berthoud Pass on August 15.

Bundy was eventually arrested in Utah as the primary suspect in a murder there, but he was extradited to Colorado where the case against him for the murder of Caryn Campbell seemed strongest. Unfortunately, the jail wasn't as strong as the case. Bundy, who'd studied law, asked to serve as his own attorney, which allowed him access to the law library at the Pitkin County Courthouse and to dress in street clothes at hearings.

During a 10:30 court recess on June 7, 1977, Bundy jumped from the library's second-story window into a flower bed. A woman passing by stopped into the courthouse and asked, "Is it normal for people to jump out of windows around here?" No, it wasn't, and Bundy was long gone.

Though they should have been more concerned that they had a serial killer in their midst, residents took it in Aspen-like stride. A restaurant offered Bundy Burgers—when you lifted the top bun, the meat had fled. One bar mixed Bundy Cocktails—equal parts rum and tequila, and two Mexican jumping beans. Meanwhile, the injured killer wandered the hills outside of town until he found a Cadillac with its keys in the ignition near the Aspen Golf Course (39551 Highway 82). Weak from lack of sleep and food, Bundy swerved through Aspen in the Caddy, and was pulled over at 2 A.M. on June 13, only blocks from the courthouse.

Bundy was tossed back into jail at the more secure Garfield County facility in Glenwood Springs. And did officials hold onto him this time? Turn to page 187 to find out.

Pitkin County Courthouse, 530 E. Main St., Aspen, CO 81611

(970) 920-5300

Hours: Always visible

Cost: Free

Directions: Main St. (Rte. 82) at Galena St.

Ready for lift-off!
Photo courtesy of Jon Barnes/The Ultimate Taxi

The Ultimate Taxi

Most people would be happy just to find a taxi without that funky smell. There is one, guaranteed, in Aspen, and it will far exceed your mildest expectations. It is the cab to beat all cabs. It is . . . the Ultimate Taxi! Launched by Jon Barnes in 1990, this local conveyance is also a recording studio, planetarium, toy store, nightclub, laser light show, and on-line performance space. This is not the kind of cab you whistle at from street corners, unless your whistle is one of admiration. No, to ride in the Ultimate Taxi you must book it in advance. And rather than order cabbie Barnes where to go, sit back while he whisks you and your friends on a tour of the town.

Aspen is one of those see-and-be-seen places, and there's no better way to get noticed than a ride in the backseat of the Ultimate Taxi with the disco ball turning. Just ask the folks who've already take a ride: George Hamilton, Ivana Trump, Peter Frampton, Ringo Starr, Bob Dole, Clint Eastwood, Hunter S. Thompson, Paula Poundstone, Melanie Griffith, and even a few people who still have careers, such as Regis Philbin and Kermit the Frog.

All Over Town, Aspen, CO 81611

(970) 927-9239

E-mail: jon@ultimatetaxi.com

Hours: Most evenings 7:30 P.M.–1 A.M.

Cost: $125 for a 40-minute group ride; includes toys, photos, and a Web page

www.ultimatetaxi.com

Directions: Call him up and have *him* do the driving.

ASPEN

Aspen boosters have long been known to exaggerate their snowfall for tourism's sake. An "Aspen foot" is a Colorado term for two inches of snow.

The ghost of a child who drowned at Aspen's Hotel Jerome (330 E. Main St., (800) 331-7213, www.hoteljerome.com) is said to haunt Room 310, which currently sits over the former pool. Witnesses claim to hear the child moaning for help.

The World's Largest Silver Nugget, weighing a whopping 1,870 pounds, was unearthed at Aspen's Smuggler Mine.

CELEBRITIES BEHAVING BADLY

Ah, Aspen! Beautiful scenery! Fabulous skiing! Celebrities acting like jerks! Here, in the closest thing Colorado has to Hollywood, the rich and famous have done their fair share of damage to themselves and others. Here's just a sampling:

John Denver, the man who epitomized the Aspen lifestyle, was arrested on August 21, 1993, for DUI in downtown Aspen. The Pitkin County court ordered him to perform a benefit concert and pay a $50 fine. One year later, *to the day*, he was busted for the same offense. This time he plowed his yellow 1963 Porsche into a tree and wound up needing 14 stitches. Prosecutors dropped the charges because his blood alcohol test was given too late to be conclusive . . . even though his BAC registered 0.10 two hours after the crash. Maybe he was drinking in the emergency room.

Singer **Claudine Longet**, former wife of **Andy Williams**, used a pistol to joke (!) with her lover, pro skier **Vladimir "Spider" Sabich**, on March 21, 1976. Unfortunately, the gun was loaded and she shot him dead. Longet was found guilty of criminally negligent homicide and spent a whopping 30 days in jail followed by two years' probation. The judge allowed her to jet off to Mexico for a one-month vacation before she went to the slammer. The jury never heard that she'd had cocaine in her system when she fired the gun, nor were they able to see her supposedly damaging diary which the sheriff conveniently lost.

Though they were specifically ordered not to by the Colorado Ski Patrol, the rambunctious Kennedy family played a game of "ski football" coming down Aspen Mountain on Copper Bowl Trail at the end of the day on December 31, 1997. **Michael Kennedy** ran into a tree and suffered massive head injuries and a severed spine. (At the time, the 39-year-old Kennedy was still trying to recover from the public disclosure that he'd had an affair with his 14-year-old babysitter.)

Cañon City
Buckskin Joe

"Gunfights and Hangings Daily!" Nooooo, this isn't a crime theme park, but a genuine fake ghost town: Buckskin Joe. (There actually *was* a Colorado mining camp named Buckskin Joe near Fairplay during the gold rush, but that ghost town is, err, *was* for real.)

This 160-acre park claims to be the largest Wild West–themed attraction in the nation, and with 11 shootouts daily, who's gonna argue? Don't worry . . . even if you've seen *Westworld*, every gun battle ends with the bad guy getting his comeuppance at the end of a hangman's noose. The effect is startlingly realistic, and just to make sure the frontier justice message comes through loud and clear—especially for the kids—they don't cut down the body until everyone who wants to pose with the swinging corpse has had the chance.

There are other, less bloody sights to see at the park: a mine, a scenic railway, a saloon, a bank, an undertaker (verrrrry important!), a candy shop . . . you get the idea. This fake town is so real that Hollywood has used it for location shots in *Cat Ballou, How the West Was Won, The Cowboys, True Grit, The Duchess and the Dirtwater Fox, The Sacketts,* and *The White Buffalo.*

1193 County Road 3A, PO Box 1387-BRO, Cañon City, CO 81215

(719) 275-5149 or (719) 275-5485

E-mail: buckskinjoe@bemail.com

Hours: Town, May–September, daily 9 A.M.–6:30 P.M.; Railway, March–December, daily 8 A.M.–8 P.M.

Cost: Adults $14, Kids (4–11) $12; Railway- or Town-only packages available

www.buckskinjoes.com

Directions: Eight miles west of town off Rte. 50.

World's Highest Suspension Bridge

Whenever you see video of some danger-seeking Colorado nut parachuting or bungee jumping off a bridge into a rocky chasm, chances are it was shot at the Royal Gorge, the World's Highest Suspension Bridge. The bridge's 1,260-foot decking stretches high over the Arkansas River, which looks like a mere trickle 1,053 feet below. The whole thing was slapped together over a quick five months in 1929, and can support more than two million pounds. Or so says the brochure.

Oddly, the bridge goes nowhere, unless you consider a snack shop, a T-shirt emporium, and a yogurt hut to be a destination. Once on the other side, you must turn around and head back. The second time across is much easier, and you barely notice the one-inch gaps between the wooden planks, offering you a clear view, past your toes, to the jagged rocks and boiling river almost a quarter mile below. And yes, in a high wind, the bridge does bounce and sway.

The park offers dozens of options to stretch out your visit if the bridge isn't enough. Take the aerial tram from rim to rim with 34 other brave souls, or ride the incline railway to the bottom of the gorge. Or, if you are the no-way-in-hell-are-you-getting-me-on-that-bridge type, you can get a great view looking *up* from the Royal Gorge Route scenic train running along the floor of the canyon . . . you wimp.

Royal Gorge Bridge and Park, 4218 County Road 3A, PO Box 549, Cañon City, CO 81215
(888) 333-5597 or (719) 275-7507
E-mail: rgb@ris.net
Hours: Daily 8:30 A.M.–Dusk
Cost: Adults $16, Kids (4–11) $13
www.royalgorgebridge.com
Directions: Twelve miles west of town on Rte. 50.

Royal Gorge Scenic Railway and Museum, 401 Water St., Cañon City, CO 81212
(888) RAILS-4-U or (303) 569-2403
E-mail: Mark@royalgorgeroute.com
Hours: May–October, daily 9 A.M., Noon, and 3 P.M.; November–April, Saturday–Sunday Noon
Cost: Adults $26.95, Kids (3–12) $16.50
www.royalgorgeroute.com
Directions: Two blocks south of Main St. between 3rd and 4th Sts.

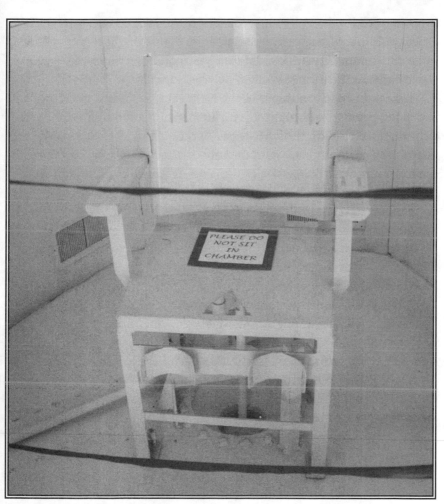

NO SITTING in the gas chamber!
Photo by author, courtesy of the Museum of Colorado Prisons

Cañon City and Florence
Prisons, Old and New

The folks in Fremont County love prisoners, mostly for economic reasons. Ever since the first territorial prison opened in Cañon City in 1871, the region has been home to the state's correctional industry. (Cañon City was offered the choice between the state college or the state penitentiary in 1868. It chose the prison because the miners thought it would be better attended.) Today, nine state and four federal institutions provide much needed local employment for residents of the county some call Criminal Inn. And just as a coastal town in Maine might have a lobster museum, Cañon City has its Museum of Colorado Prisons.

Housed in the former Women's Correctional Institution, Cellhouse 4, it's the only prison museum in the nation that is located adjacent to an active Big House. That's right, as you approach the building's front gate, a tall stone wall rises on the left, topped by a watchtower with a gun-toting guard. If that doesn't get you in the mood, perhaps the gas chamber in the front yard will. Thirty-two criminals were gassed in Colorado between 1933 and 1967, but only the last eight died in this chamber. Step on in and read the sign: "Please Do Not Sit in Chamber." The only seat is a chair with arm and leg irons.

Inside the museum, each tiny cell houses a different display. In one you'll see a collection of homemade weapons confiscated from prisoners and now encased in Plexiglas. In another, there's a variety of "inmate control devices": clubs, tear gas, electric prods, and the Old Gray Mare, a flogging horse that was popular (with the guards) until the 1950s. Next, see the rope used in the prison's last hanging (December 1, 1933). You'll find it near a scale model of a modern lethal injection table.

During your visit, you'll learn about an October 1929 riot in which eight guards and five inmates died, including instigator A. A. "Danny" Daniels. See items related to cannibal Alferd Packer's stay in Cañon City. Check out the replica of the isolation unit known as Little Siberia. Through it all, if there's one message that comes across loud and clear, it's that crime doesn't pay . . . except at the gift shop.

Museum of Colorado Prisons, 201 N. First St., PO Box 1229, Cañon City, CO 81215
(719) 269-3015
E-mail: curator@prisonmuseum.org
Hours: May–August, daily 8:30 A.M.–6 P.M.; September–April, Friday–Sunday daily
   10 A.M.–5 P.M.
Cost: Adults $5, Seniors (65+) $4, Kids (6–12) $3
www.prisonmuseum.org
Directions: On the southwest side of town, at First and Macon Sts.

The correctional facilities around Cañon City support a wide spectrum of criminals, from petty thieves to the worst of the worst. The fed's Administrative Maximum Facility, or ADX, houses, or has housed, some of the nation's most notorious killers. Theodore Kaczynski, the Unabomber, and Timothy McVeigh are former residents. They were eventually transferred to Terre Haute, Indiana, where the federal death chamber is located . . . and everyone knows what happened to Timmy. Ramzi Yousef, who bombed the World Trade Center the first time, and Terry Nichols, McVeigh's conspirator, are current and very permanent ADX guests.

ADX Federal Penitentiary, 5880 State Highway 67, PO Box 8500, Florence, CO 81226

(719) 784-9454

Hours: Always visible

Cost: Free

www.bop.gov/facilnot.html

Directions: South of Siloam Rd. on Rte. 67.

Central City
The Lady in Black

Ghosts have the reputations of being undependable. Like taking your car to a mechanic, the moment you convince somebody to take a look, the rattle stops. But the Lady in Black is an exception. Central City's most famous graveyard spirit shows herself on November 1 and April 5 every year.

She is believed to be the jilted lover, or widowed fiancée, of John Edward Cameron, a 28-year-old town fireman who died suddenly on November 1, 1887. The woman attended his funeral (as flesh and blood) and placed a bouquet of columbines on his fresh grave. She still does these days, but as a ghost.

Central City encourages ghost hunters to explore its pioneer cemeteries. On the third Saturday of October each year (at 2 P.M.) the Historical Society hosts a Cemetery Crawl at one of the town's 11 graveyards. Costumed actors hang around the tombstones and portray the speechless residents below their feet.

Masonic Cemetery, Nevada St., Central City, CO 80427

No phone

Hours: Tombstone always visible; Ghost on November 1 and April 5

Cost: Free

www.centralcitycolorado.net

Directions: Head west out of town on Nevada St.; it's just past the casino parking lot.

Sometimes size *does* matter.

Conifer
Eat in a Hot Dog

Sometimes size *does* matter. Unlike Los Angeles' famous Tail o' the Pup hot dog stand, 10 people can actually eat *inside* this giant wiener, a fact that allows it to stay open year-round. Conifer's 42-foot, 14-ton hot dog was built in 1966 by Marcus Shannon, and was originally located in Denver (on W. Colfax, near St. Anthony Hospital). The dog was moved up into the mountains in 1969 when developers threatened to bulldoze it. Jealous bastards!

Many folks in Conifer, a nature-loving bunch, were not entirely thrilled with their new frankfurter and some tried to prevent its relocation. Thank God they lost. Today the hot dog is a local landmark, but it's still not safe. Once again, developers are out to chomp this wiener. The structure was put up for sale in 1999 for $300,000, which sounds steep until you hear what they were asking for the land it sits on: $695,000. No takers yet for the million-dollar dog, but you'd better see it while you can.

Coney Island Dairy Land, 25877 Conifer Rd., Conifer, CO 80433

(303) 838-4210

Hours: Always visible; Open 9:30 A.M.–7 P.M.

Cost: Meals $3–$5

Directions: At the east end of Conifer, just north of Rte. 285.

AVON
When challenged to name the town's newest bridge, the Avon Town Council dubbed it Bob. The town celebrates with a Bob the Bridge Festival each year.

BRECKENRIDGE
The town of Breckinridge was changed to Breckenridge when then–vice president **John C. Breckenridge** supported the Confederate cause during the Civil War.

CAÑON CITY
Cañon City's name was almost changed to Oreodelphia in its early days.

CENTRAL CITY
The famous "Face on the Barroom Floor" is still on the floor of Central City's Teller House (120 Eureka St., (303) 582-3200. It was painted by newspaperman Herndon Davis in 1936.

"Another class is too largely represented [in Central City], composed of effeminate clerks. Every vacancy is filled, and they know it well, yet they persist in standing idle all the day, loafing at the street corners, impressing the superficial traveler that times are dull in Colorado."
—H. M. Stanley

Creede
Bob Ford Gets His

Bob Ford, "the dirty little coward who shot Mr. Howard," was not a popular guy. You see, Mr. Howard was really an alias used by Jesse James, a man who had kindly taken in Bob Ford and his brother Charley to show them the bank-robbin' ropes. But the Fords were more interested in collecting the $10,000 reward put up by the Missouri governor. On April 3, 1882, Bob Ford shot James in the forehead at James's St. Joseph, Missouri, home. Instead of getting the reward, the Fords were arrested, tried, and convicted of murder, but they were pardoned by the governor before being put to death.

It was an open secret that the James family wanted these two varmints dead. Charley, unnerved by constantly looking over his shoulder, committed suicide in May 1884. Bob headed west and ended up in the mining town of Creede in 1892, opening a gambling hall called the Creede Exchange. For a variety of reasons, Ford didn't immediately make many friends in Creede. He went on a drunken shooting rampage through the town in April; threatened to burn the town down after a vigilante committee dubbed "The Hundred" warned him to leave, and he didn't; and was associated with a bunch of hoodlums who really did burn down the town in early June.

Undeterred by the threats, Ford pitched a tent in the ashes. It was located roughly where the boulder adjacent to the Visitor's Information Bureau at the Art Park on Main Street. His tent was the smoldering town's only dance hall and bar, and on opening day, it was packed. But Ford's success didn't last long. One day, actually.

On June 8, 1892, Edward O. "Red" Kelly entered Ford's dance hall with a loaded shotgun, placed the barrels to Ford's head, and pulled both triggers. Why? The widely repeated story was that there was bad blood between Ford and Kelly over a stolen diamond ring, but that wasn't the case. Kelly was married to a relative of the Younger Gang who, years earlier, had ridden with James robbing banks in the Midwest. The James family reportedly paid Kelly $5,000 for the job, and Creede con man "Soapy" Smith assisted by bringing Kelly to town. Kelly was convicted of second-degree murder and served 10 years in Cañon City before being pardoned by the governor.

Ford was buried in Creede's Sunnyside Cemetery in a service attended by Frank James, Jesse's brother, who just happened to be in the neighborhood at the time of the murder. Ford's widow had Bob dug up and taken back to Richmond, Missouri, three months later. Today, his empty grave is still marked.

Sunnyside Cemetery, Bachelor Rd., Creede, CO 81130

Contact: Creede/Mineral County Chamber of Commerce, PO Box 580, Creede, CO 81130

(800) 327-2102 or (719) 658-2374

E-mail: creede@amigo.net

Hours: Always visible

Cost: Free

www.creede-co.com/cr_history.html

Directions: At the south end of town; follow the signs.

CENTRAL CITY

Much of Central City burned to the ground in 1874, supposedly after Chinese residents touched off a blaze with their New Year's fireworks. True or not, other folks used it as an excuse to drive the Chinese out of their smoldering town.

CREEDE

"It's day all day in the daytime, and there is no night in Creede."
—Popular observation in the rip-roaring mining days of Creede

CRESTED BUTTE

Fifty-nine miners died in an explosion at the Jokerville Mine near Crested Butte on January 24, 1884.

CRESTONE

Journalist **Bill Moyers** claimed he saw a bush burst into flames—not unlike the one Moses saw—while hiking in the hills near Crestone.

Kind of like the Bat Cave.

Underground Firehouse

Creede is a town that appreciates its heritage: hard rock mining. So when it came time to build a new firehouse, local miners volunteered to blast it out of a cliff along Willow Creek Road. The firehouse opened in 1982 (blasting started in 1976). It is the World's Only Underground Firehouse. Each of the town's fire trucks has its own rock stall burrowed at a 45-degree angle from the central bore, which extends 139 feet into the cliff. The entrance is secured by a large garage door.

With this modern facility, Creede won't have to worry about conflagrations like the one that wiped out the entire town in 1892. Even if the rest of the town burns, the fire station will survive. If you want to tour the Creede Underground Firehouse, come in the summer when 4H volunteers are giving tours.

Willow Creek Rd., PO Box 432, Creede, CO 81130

(719) 658-0811

Hours: Call for tour

Cost: Free

www.creede.com/page10.html

Directions: At the north end of town, opposite the dam, next to the Underground Mining Museum.

Cripple Creek
The Old Homestead

It's not often that you see a museum dedicated to a whorehouse, and isn't that a shame? The Old Homestead's name suggests mom and apple pie but belies the building's true identity as Cripple Creek's classiest brothels. It was founded by madam Pearl DeVere who wanted a Parisian style bordello in the heart of the Rockies.

Myers Avenue had long been the mining camp's red-light district. Carry Nation called the street a "foul cesspool." However, the 10-room Old Homestead was anything but. Pearl's girls wore gowns, and no patron was admitted without a written application. The women were "courted" in three parlors while they sat on cupid-back chairs until the right man, with the right amount of money and references, came along. Today the museum has placed mannequins in the chairs to give the place an authentic feel.

When Pearl died of a morphine overdose in 1897, she was buried in Mt. Pisgah Cemetery under a heart-shaped wooden marker. It was later replaced with a marble tombstone, also heart-shaped. The stones covering her plot were placed there by thankful miners.

Myers Avenue's activity outlasted Pearl, and in 1914 was criticized in an article by New York writer Julian Street. Upon reading it, tourism picked up, and locals wanted to rename the avenue Julian Street in the prude's honor.

353 E. Myers Ave., Cripple Creek, CO 80813

(719) 689-3090

E-mail: oldhomemuseum@cs.com

Hours: June–September, daily 10 A.M.–4 P.M., Saturday–Sunday 11 A.M.–4 P.M.; May, Saturday–Sunday 10 A.M.–5 P.M.

Cost: Adults $3, Kids (10–13) $1.50

www.cripple-creek.co.us/homestead.htm

Directions: One block south of Bennett St. (Rte. 67), between 3rd and 4th Sts.

Mt. Pisgah Cemetery, Rte. 1, Cripple Creek, CO 80813

Cemetery Tours: (719) 689-9113

Hours: Always visible

Cost: Free

Directions: Head northwest out of town on Bennett Ave. (Teller County Rte. 1). The cemetery is on the left.

A REGULAR HO'-DOWN

T. J. Flournoy, the stuffed rooster mascot of the Chicken Ranch of LaGrange, Texas, was homeless after the infamous whorehouse was shut down in the 1970s. He has found a new home at the Imperial Hotel Casino's Red Rooster Bar (123 Bennett Ave. (719) 689-7777) in Cripple Creek.

Each year, on the third Saturday in June, the town of Central City celebrates **Madam Lou Bunch Days** to honor its most celebrated brothel manager. Festival events include a bed race, a costume contest, and a dance.

Mount Silverheels, northwest of Fairplay, is named after a dance-hall girl known first by miners for her silver dancing slippers, but later for nursing smallpox victims during an 1863 epidemic. The once-ravishing beauty was also stricken, but survived, and then disappeared, presumably so nobody would have to look at her disfigured face. The miners honored their heroine with a mountain.

The **Mattie Silks Building** in Denver (2009 Market St.) was once among the town's better-known brothels. That should come as no surprise; Mattie Silks was once among the town's better-known madams. The Denver Planning Board was duped into thinking the building was Silks's residence, and granted Landmark status to the building in 1981 as an example of nineteenth-century architecture.

One block away, another house that Mattie ran, the House of Mirrors, has been converted into a fancy restaurant of the same name. In addition to fine food, **Mattie's House of Mirrors** (1942–46 Market St., (303) 297-9600) features a collection of photographs from the building's heyday.

Next door, the Silver Dollar Hotel started as a bordello, but later became a skid-row flophouse. Finally, it was converted to what has become Denver's best-known jazz club, **El Chapultepec** (1962 Market St., (303) 295-9126). Bill Clinton stopped by during a campaign swing and ended up playing a few licks on a borrowed sax. Maybe he needs to update his address book.

Drake
Big Thompson Canyon

Considering the day the Big Thompson flood occurred, you might think Mother Nature had a bone to pick with the state of Colorado. The day before the Centennial State's centennial on July 31, 1976, a freak thunderstorm dumped 12 inches of rain in four hours and sent a 20-foot wall of the water down the Big Thompson Canyon, flushing out everything in its path. Because of the upcoming Colorado Day celebrations, campers were packed in along the river. In all, 139 folks perished. Six of them were never found. More than 400 homes were destroyed.

Today, as you drive through Big Thompson Canyon between Loveland and Estes Park, you'll see many "Climb to Safety" signs. Believe them. A monument to the victims stands at the Miller Fork convergence along the river, where the old town of Drake once stood, and where the new town of Drake stands today.

Route 34, Drake, CO 80515

No phone

Hours: Always visible

Cost: Free

Directions: Along Rte. 34.

Empire
The Original Hard Rock Cafe

It's not what you think. When they say "hard" rock in Empire, they mean *hard* rock. Not rock 'n' roll rock. Rock rock. This eatery opened in 1930 as the Empire Cafe, but changed to the Hard Rock Cafe two years later, back when Mick Jagger was just a teenager.

Then, some 40 years later in 1971, another Hard Rock Cafe opened in London. Slowly but surely they launched new eateries all over the globe. Their goal: world domination. Fearing he would be unable to fight a mighty British conglomerate, the Empire Hard Rock Cafe's owner signed over the name to the town. Empire's town offices were located upstairs, in the same 1898 building as the cafe. Faced with fighting City Hall, the Brits dropped their threats.

Don't be disappointed when you aren't able to see U2's sunglasses or Madonna's pointy bra here. They do, however, have a nice display case with ore samples and mineral specimens.

203 G St., Empire, CO 80438

No phone

Hours: Monday–Friday, 7 A.M.–6 P.M., Saturday–Sunday 7 A.M.–8 P.M.

Cost: Meals $3–$6

Directions: At the west end of town, off Rte. 40.

CRIPPLE CREEK

Cripple Creek was once known as Poverty Gulch before being changed to Fremont. It was then changed to Cripple Creek to honor the infamous cattle-crippling creek running through town.

Cripple Creek's newspaper, *The Gusher*, was printed with gold ink in 1891.

Cripple Creek was destroyed by a fire started during a barroom brawl on April 25, 1896. The buildings left standing were later leveled when a grease fire in an unharmed hotel ignited a dynamite storage shed.

Thirteen miners were killed by a bomb at the Independence Mine near Cripple Creek during labor unrest in 1904.

Estes Park
America's Highest Continuous Road

Trail Ridge Road is the nation's highest continuous highway, and as such, is only open part of the year. Snow removal crews work feverishly to open the road for Memorial Day weekend, and most of the time they succeed. However, the view you'll get in June will be mostly of snow, snow, and more snow as you cut through drifts that are often taller than your car. You're better off waiting until late summer.

When you reach the 12,183-foot summit, stop in at the Alpine Visitor's Center, or take a stroll up the Tundra Nature Trail. But take it easy; this altitude is a dream come true for a cardiologist's accountant. They don't call this the Tombstone Ridge for nothing.

Incidentally, the nation's highest paved road is to the top of Colorado's Mount Evans. However, once you reach the peak, you have to return down the same way you came up.

Trail Ridge Rd., Rocky Mountain National Park, Rte. 34, Estes Park, CO 80517

(970) 586-1206

Hours: Always open, summer only; Alpine Visitors Center, June–August, daily 10 A.M.– 4:30 P.M.

Cost: Free

www.nps.gov/romo

Directions: West of Estes Park on Rte. 34, heading toward Grand Lake.

Baldpate Inn Key Room

One of the keys to a successful hotel or restaurant is a gimmick, and at the Baldpate Inn, the key is keys. Lots and lots of keys. Eighty-some years ago, the owners of this mountaintop retreat were convinced by author Earl Derr Biggers that their hotel had roughly the same layout as the setting for his mystery novel, *The Seven Keys of Baldpate*. Gordon and Ethel Mace named their establishment the Baldpate Inn and made a set of seven keys its logo. Then, in 1923, lawyer Clarence Darrow suggested that the inn start a key collection. The Key Room was born.

To date, the Baldpate Inn has collected more than 12,000 keys, but it's been a long time since they've counted them. If you look long enough, you can find keys to:

- Mozart's wine cellar
- the very first bank robbed by Jesse James

- the White House
- Hitler's desk and Berchstegaden bomb shelter
- Westminster Abbey
- Buckingham Palace
- Frankenstein Castle
- the Chicago lab where the atomic bomb was invented
- "My Old Kentucky Home"
- the Waldorf-Astoria Hotel
- the Stanley Hotel room where Stephen King wrote *The Shining*
- Jack Benny's dressing room at Paramount Studios
- Fort Knox
- a sardine can
- the pre-explosion *Challenger* Space Shuttle bay doors
- the Naussau County, New York, Sludge Dumping Facility
- Edgar Allen Poe's University of Virginia dormitory room . . . number 13!

Understand that many, if not all, of these locks have long since been changed, so you won't be able to nab the White House key and let yourself in the next time you visit Washington. And finally, if you'd like to contribute a key to the collection, feel free to bring one along—they're always looking for more.

4900 Highway 7, PO Box 4445, Estes Park, CO 80517

(866) 577-KEYS or (970) 586-KEYS

E-mail: baldpatein@aol.com

Hours: Late May–October, daily 9 A.M.–8 P.M.

Cost: Free

www.BaldpateInn.com

Directions: Seven miles south of town on Rte. 7, just north of the Lily Lake Visitors Center.

EMPIRE
Empire claims to be the "Hummingbird Capital of the World."

ESTES PARK
When the Lawn Lake dam burst on July 15, 1982, it sent a wall of water and mud through downtown Estes Park, killing two people.

The Shining Hotel

You know the story: a mild-mannered caretaker at a snowbound mountain lodge gets cabin fever (in spades!), talks to evil spirits, tries to chop his wife and clairvoyant son into pieces with an ax, and freezes to death in a blizzard. Stephen King came up with the tale during on a visit to the Stanley Hotel on the last day of the 1973 season. On that night, King and his wife were the only guests, but after chatting with a spectral bartender, seeing a pair of Victorian ghost girls, discovering a dead body in the tub, and watching an elevator empty its cargo of human blood, King realized, "Now *this* would make a great book!"

Well, not *all* of that happened at the Stanley. Mostly King just spent the night in Room 217, dreaming up the spooky tale. Today, horror fans request the "REDRUM Room" when they visit, though for reasons obvious to those familiar with the book or movie, the Stanley has not named the suite that. In fact, the hotel doesn't even have its number plate since King fans keep ripping it off as a souvenir.

The Stanley Hotel was opened in 1909 by Freelan Stanley, inventor of the Stanley Steamer. He had come west to be cured of his tuberculosis, fell in love with the mountains, and built the hotel with his twin brother Francis. Many famous guests have stayed at the Stanley over the years—Teddy Roosevelt, John Phillip Sousa, Molly Brown, Bob Dylan—but none of them profited from the experience as much as King did.

Freelan Stanley eventually succumbed to TB. Some say his ghost is still here, and sometimes plays the Steinway in the music room. That's about all you're likely to experience from the other side here.

The Stanley Hotel, Room 217, 333 Wonderview Dr., PO Box 1767, Estes Park, CO 80517

(800) 976-1377 or (970) 586-3371

Hours: Always open

Cost: $159/night and up

www.stanleyhotel.com

Directions: Just north of the intersection of Rtes. 34 and 36.

EVERGREEN

Would-be presidential assassin **John Hinkley, Jr.**, grew up on Brookline Rd., near Medinah Dr., in Evergreen.

Evergreen
International Bell Museum

This museum is for ding dongs, and no, I don't mean those tasty foil-wrapped Hostess treats. I mean bells of all shapes, sizes, and sounds—more than 6,000 in all. They're the collection of Winston Jones, curator of this home-based museum. During your personal tour you'll be told of all the uses for bells throughout the ages, mostly to signal others, but sometimes to drive them crazy. You'll also see clangers once owned by celebrities such as Harry Houdini, Amelia Earhart, Sarah Bernhardt, and Lillian Russell.

30213 Upper Bear Creek Canyon Rd., PO Box 1601, Evergreen, CO 80439

(303) 674-3422

Hours: May–September, Tuesday–Sunday 10 A.M.–5 P.M., by appointment only

Cost: Adults $4, Kids $2

Directions: One mile west of town toward Troutdale.

FRASER
Fraser sometimes calls itself the Icebox of the Nation.

GARFIELD
Eight people were killed when a school bus careened down Monarch Pass and crashed near Garfield on September 11, 1971. Most victims were members of the Gunnison Junior High football team.

GEORGETOWN
Thirty-one people died when a flight chartered by the Wichita State University football team crashed into Mount Bethel near Georgetown on October 2, 1970.

GILETTE
The town of Gilette hosted the state's first, and only, bullfight in 1895.

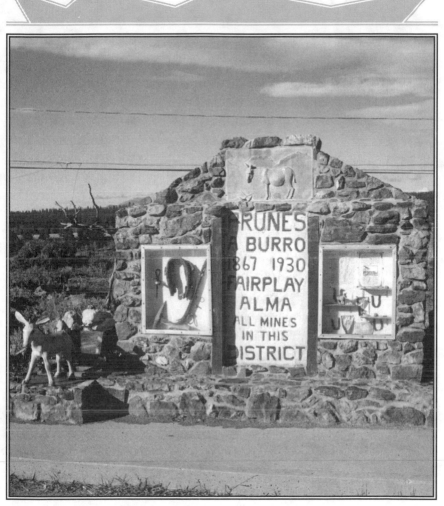

Prunes was an ass.

Fairplay
A Couple of Asses

Prunes and Shorty were a pair of asses. Well, *burros* actually, sometimes called Rocky Mountain canaries in these parts.

A miner's burro was the equivalent of a modern-day pickup truck. Prunes was owned by Rupe Sherwood, and over the course of 50-some years worked most of the mines around South Park. When Prunes became too old to pull ore carts, he was freed to roam the streets of Fairplay, begging for food from its all-too-generous residents. This resulted in an unfortunate accident when the burro was trapped for several days in an abandoned shack during a 1930 blizzard. By the time Prunes was discovered, he was too weak to go on, and had to be destroyed.

The miners who loved Prunes laid him to rest on the town's main street and erected a monument over the grave. It contains some of Prunes's gear and ore samples from the mines he worked. When Rupe Sherwood died a year later, his cremated remains were buried just behind the memorial.

Unlike his much-honored predecessor, Shorty the burro started as a freeloader, and never worked a day in his life. Still, the folks here loved him. When Shorty died, his furry pal Bum (a dog) laid down on his grave and refused to eat. Bum died shortly thereafter. The folks of Fairplay reopened Shorty's grave and dumped Bum in. A monument to Shorty now stands on the courthouse square.

Prunes's Monument, 529 Front St., Fairplay, CO 80440

No phone

Hours: Always visible

Cost: Free

Directions: Next to the Hand Hotel, between 5th and 6th Sts., on the south side of town.

Shorty's Monument, Courthouse Lawn, 640 Hathaway St., Fairplay, CO 80440

No phone

Hours: Always visible

Cost: Free

Directions: At 7th and Hathaway Sts., next to South Park Junior-Senior High School.

IF YOU LIKE DONKEYS . . .
Colorado hosts two donkey races each year. On the fourth weekend in June, Cripple Creek celebrates **Donkey Derby Days**, an event that includes the Pack Burro Race. Fairplay has its own event on the last weekend in July. **The Burro Days Race** pits runners and their burros in a 31-mile jog over Mosquito Pass. The race motto? "Get Your Ass Over the Pass."

The Real South Park

Fairplay has the unique distinction of being the Colorado town most often seen in the popular media today, and yet, few people have ever heard of it. Considering the way it is portrayed, maybe that's for the best. Fairplay was once known as South Park City, and though creators Matt Stone and Trey Parker might deny it, they based their bad-taste cartoon here.

Perhaps Parker and Stone chose Fairplay because it is the closest town to the geographic center of the state. Perhaps it was just a dart thrown at a map. Fans of the raunchy cartoon will likely enjoy driving around town giggling at places like South Park High School and South Park Plumbing and Heating. On the southwest side of town is a mining camp museum called South Park City where visitors can buy authentic Comedy Central souvenirs.

South Park City Museum, 100 Fourth St., PO Box 634, Fairplay, CO 80440

(719) 836-2387

Hours: May, September–October, daily 9 A.M.–5 P.M.; June–August, daily 9 A.M.–7 P.M.

Cost: Adults $5, Seniors $4, Kids (6–12) $2

www.coloradodirectory.com/southparkmuseum/

Directions: One block south of Rte. 9 as it heads west out of town.

Florissant
World's Largest Petrified Stump

The area around Florissant is a beautiful mountain park, but if you'd been here 35 million years ago, it was a real mess. Around that time, give or take a million years, a volcano belched forth a column of ash and cinders that buried Lake Florissant and all that lived nearby. Though it proved the undoing of a redwood forest, it established the ideal conditions for fossil formation. Everything from fragile insects to tree stumps has been unearthed here, the largest example being a redwood that was 13 feet in diameter at the base.

Unfortunately, when the fossil beds were first discovered, this was privately held land. The owner set up a mine-your-own-fossils tourist trap where paying visitors were encouraged to take home any samples they found. The federal government purchased the site in 1969 to preserve what remained of the fossils. Most of the best stuff is located in the Visitor Center.

Florissant Fossil Beds National Monument, 15807 Teller County Rd. 1, PO Box 185, Florissant, CO 80816

(719) 748-3253

E-mail: jean_rodeck@nps.gov

Hours: June–August, daily 8 A.M.–7 P.M.; September–May, 8 A.M.–4:30 P.M.

Cost: Summers Adults $2, Kids Free; Winters Free

www.nps.gov/flfo

Directions: South on Rte. 1 from Rte. 24 at Florissant.

Gunnison
World's Largest W

Let there be no mistake: when you're in Gunnison, you're in Western country. Western State, that is. If you need any proof, just look to the mountains and behold the mighty *W* on the side of Smelter Hill.

It hasn't always been this way; the college was founded as the State Normal College. Dr. John Johnson suggested students put an *N* on the hill in 1915, which they did, and it remained until the college was renamed.

Western State's president declared May 2, 1923, a one-time holiday to change the *N* to a *W*. To maintain the glory of the alphabet's 23rd letter, the *W* is repainted every year during homecoming. There was some talk of dismantling the 400-by-350-foot eyesore back in the 1970s, but that plan was scuttled when it was determined that they'd do more environmental damage by removing it than by leaving it as it was.

Smelter Hill, Gunnison, CO 81231

No phone

Hours: Daylight

Cost: Free

www.western.edu

Directions: Easily visible from the Western campus.

GUNNISON

Gunnison has the lowest average temperature of any town in the continental United States.

E.T. phone here.
Photo by author, courtesy of the UFO Watchtower

Hooper
UFO Watchtower

Judy Messoline will tell you: seeing is believing. She admits that when she opened her UFO Watchtower a few years back, she was mostly trying to capitalize on local interest in UFOs. The San Luis Valley has long been a hotbed of unusual activity, so her TLC ranch seemed the perfect location for a space-themed gift shop. She erected a large, 10-foot-high metal platform around a half-dome structure which she filled with alien toys, books, and T-shirts. She then hung out her shingle on Route 17.

Soon strange things started to happen in the skies over her watch-tower. Things like falling stars that somehow never reached the ground, but hovered before impact. Cigar-shaped craft buzzed the valley floor. Folks who'd claimed they'd been abducted started frequenting her adjacent campground. Messoline converted to the "something's out there" camp.

The UFO Watchtower is a fun place to visit, even for nonbelievers. Cutouts of little green men and women affixed to fence posts are perfect for gag photos. The gift shop has a nice selection of souvenirs. And the watchtower platform offers a clear panoramic view of the mysterious valley. Be sure to check your watch before and after your visit. If you

Take me to your Watchtower.

notice that you've lost a few hours you can't account for, chances are you've joined the ranks of the abductees' club.

Route 17, PO Box 583, Hooper, CO 81136

(719) 378-2296 or (719) 378-2271

E-mail: judy@ufowatchtower.com

Hours: June–September, daily 11 A.M.–10 P.M.; September–May, Friday–Saturday 1 P.M.–Dark

Cost: Free; donations encouraged

www.ufowatchtower.com

Directions: Two and a half miles north of Hooper on Rte. 17.

ANOTHER UFO WATCHTOWER?

Drivers along I-70 near Genessee, west of Denver, will notice a clam-shaped building atop a mountain on the south side of the highway. Another UFO watchtower? No, just the 1963 Sculpture House, designed and partially constructed by architect Charles Deaton. Moviegoers might have seen it in *Sleeper* and *For Your Eyes Only*. It was recently purchased and construction was completed. It is privately owned.

Keeping the funny pages safe for democracy!

Idaho Springs
Steve Canyon Statue
Steve Canyon was a true hero in World War II: he valiantly battled the Axis every day, and even more on Sundays, and still found time to raise money for War Bonds. Sure, he fought from newspapers' funny pages, but he saw as much combat as Ronald Reagan.

Canyon was the creation of cartoonist Milt Caniff. Folks in Idaho Springs were so impressed by the character's war efforts that they successfully petitioned the Colorado legislature to change the name of nearby Squirrel Gulch to Steve Canyon. A life-size statue was commissioned, and the federal government honored Canyon with a plaque: "The United States Treasury salutes Steve Canyon and through him, all American cartoon characters who serve the nation." I guess that rules out those Katzenjammer Kids!

Idaho Springs Visitors Center, 2060 Miner St., Idaho Springs, CO 80452

No phone

Hours: Always visible

Cost: Free

Directions: East of the Visitor's Center at 23rd St.

A Packer picnic.

Lake City
Alferd Packer, Man Eater

Lured by the prospect of silver near Breckenridge, Colorado, Alferd Packer and 20 others left Provo, Utah, on November 8, 1873, heading east. Packer had convinced the group he was a competent guide to the region, enough so that they bailed him out of a Salt Lake City jail where he was being held on counterfeiting charges.

And what a guide Packer turned out to be! The original group got as far as Chief Ouray's encampment near present-day Delta in late January before the winter snows got too deep. The chief advised them against pressing on, but six decided to proceed anyway on February 9, 1874. It was a decision five would regret.

About two miles south of present-day Lake City, the party was snowbound and hungry. Exactly what happened next is still up for debate. If you believe Alferd Packer's third version of events, he was off trying to rustle up some grub when Wilson Bell killed Israel Swan, Frank Miller, George Noon, and James Humphreys with an ax. Packer returned to find Bell hunched over a campfire, chowing down on his victims. The murderer lunged at Packer who then shot him dead. Not one to let good meat go to waste, Packer ate pieces of his former companions until the weather cleared up enough for him to continue on.

On April 16, 1874, Packer stumbled into the Los Piños Indian Agency, 25 miles south of Gunnison. Refusing food (which seemed odd) he told a harrowing tale of being abandoned by his party and subsisting on a diet of roots and rose buds, though it sounded fishy. A Ute Indian in the agency at the time was said to observe, "Him too fat." After regaining his strength, Packer continued on to Saguache. There he spent money freely on booze and gambling, and related his false exploits to anyone who would listen.

Meanwhile, back in Los Piños, another party stumbled into the agency, a group of men who had traveled with Packer as far as Delta, and doubted his story. Where did he get that Winchester rifle and all that money? Word was sent to Saguache to arrest Packer and bring him back to Los Piños for questioning.

Now Packer began singing a different tune. His second story had four of his companions murdering Swan (while Packer was looking for firewood) and eating his flesh. The party pressed on, and Humphreys died. They ate him, too, and kept moving. A week later (again, while Packer was looking for firewood) Miller was killed. Packer remembered Miller was good eating because he was from fat German stock. Farther along the trail, Bell shot Noon. As one of two survivors, Packer shot Bell twice after the latter tried to make him into his next meal.

When Packer couldn't lead the Los Piños authorities to the site of the final killing, he was locked up in the Saguache jail (405 Eighth St.).

Then, completely by accident, *Harper's Weekly* artist John A. Randolph and a group of searchers stumbled across the corpse-strewn encampment near Lake San Cristobal, and Packer found himself in very big trouble. Fortunately for him, he escaped three days before the word got to Saguache. He used a key slipped to him by (rumors say) town founder Otto Mears who was fearful of bad publicity.

Packer Massacre Site, Rte. 149, Lake City, CO 81235

No phone

Hours: Always visible

Cost: Free

Directions: Head toward Slumgullion Pass on Rte. 149, on the north side of the road just past the Lake Fork of the Gunnison River bridge.

Packer was captured in Fort Fetterman, Wyoming, on March 12, 1883, nine years after his escape. He was living under the alias John Schwartze. He wasn't identified by his face, but by his telltale high-pitched voice. A member of the original Provo party, Frenchy Cabazon, recognized Packer's whiny tone in a bar one night. Packer was returned to Lake City to stand trail.

Found guilty on one count of murder (for Swan) on Friday, April 13, 1883, Packer was sentenced to die on May 19. He was granted a stay of execution while the constitutionality of the statute pertaining to the case was determined. Packer spent his days in the Gunnison jail braiding watch chains from his own hair for fascinated tourists.

The Hinsdale County Courthouse is still used today for trials, though exciting courtroom dramas are less frequent than they used to be. If you stop by when it's open, you're welcome to take a look around and see a copy of the court transcripts opened (and under glass) to a page inked during the court's most famous trial.

Hinsdale County Courthouse, 311 N. Henson St., Lake City, CO 81235

(970) 944-2227

Hours: Monday–Friday 9 A.M.–4 P.M.

Cost: Free

www.lakecityco.com

Directions: Between Third and Fourth Sts., one block east of Rte. 149 (Gunnison Ave.) in the center of town.

All I need is some fava beans and a nice Chianti . . .
Photo courtesy of the Colorado Historical Society, F-3823

Because of the difference between the territorial law in 1874 (when the murders were committed) and the state law in 1883 (under which he'd been tried), Packer's conviction was thrown out in 1886 and a new trial was ordered. It took place at the Gunnison County Courthouse. This time Packer was convicted on five counts of manslaughter and sentenced to five consecutive eight-year terms in Cañon City. (See Colorado Territorial Prison, page 115)

Outgoing Colorado governor Charles Thomas, in his last official act, pardoned Packer on January 10, 1901, for health considerations. (To follow the man-eater's final years, see page 34.)

The repository for Packeriana is the Hinsdale County Museum in Lake City. They've got a cute dollhouse he made while a prisoner in Cañon City, complete with a rag doll resembling the cannibal, as well as leg irons once used to restrain him and metal buttons found with his victims' bodies. They've also got Packer refrigerator magnets, lapel buttons, and other trinkets for sale.

A chunk of Frank Miller's skull and a rusty gun with three bullets still in the chamber—which is believed to have been used by Packer to shoot Shannon Bell—are currently in the collection of the Museum of Western Colorado (5th & Ute Sts., Grand Junction (970) 242-0971). These artifacts were unearthed in July 1989 when the victims' bodies were dug up for forensic analysis. Surprisingly, wounds on the bones corroborated elements of Packer's account of events. The remains were reburied.

And there's more. For a truly tasteless meal, visit the Alferd Packer Memorial Grill at the University of Colorado Memorial Center in Boulder (Euclid & Broadway, www.colorado.edu/food/grill_pages) where you can buy an El Canibal burrito. Students once hosted an annual "Packer Snacker," a kind of a springtime eating Olympics. It is no longer celebrated. A statue of the cannibal was placed at the student union in 1982. Not-yet-famous CU students Trey Parker and Matt Stone made a film, *Cannibal! The Musical,* in 1993 and sent it to the Sundance Film Festival. It was not accepted.

Hinsdale County Museum, 130 Silver St., PO Box 353, Lake City, CO 81235

(970) 944-9515

E-mail: museum@lakecity.net

Hours: June–September, Monday–Friday 10 A.M.–4 P.M., Saturday–Sunday 1–4 P.M.

Cost: Adults $2, Kids (under 12) 50¢

members.dencity.com/dw/HCHS/museum3.html

Directions: At Second St., one block west of Rte. 149 (Gunnison Ave.) at the south end of town.

THE MOST FAMOUS COLORADO QUOTE NEVER UTTERED

"There were only seven Democrats in all of Hinsdale County and you, you man-eatin' son of a bitch, you ate five of them! I sentence you to be hanged by the neck until you're dead, dead, dead for reducing the Democrat population of the state. I would sentence you to hell, but the statutes forbid it!"

This quote, or one like it, has long been attributed to presiding Judge Melville B. Gerry. But the statement was, in fact, uttered by saloon keeper Larry Dolan and falsely attributed to the elected Democrat. Dolan owned the Saguache saloon where Packer first started throwing around his ill-gotten money in 1874 after coming down from the mountains. He later moved to Lake City and opened the Centennial Saloon, and testified at Packer's trial.

Gerry did offer an eloquent summary during the trial's sentencing phase, where he said, in part, "As the days come and go and the years of your pilgrimage go by, the memory of you and your crimes will fade from the minds of men."

Fat chance.

Leadville
America's Highest City

At an average elevation of 10,152 feet, just shy of two miles above sea level, Leadville is the highest incorporated city in the nation. This hasn't always been the case; other Colorado settlements were even higher during the gold and silver rushes, like Animas Forks at 11,584 feet, but are currently ghost towns.

What does the altitude get Leadvillians besides brief mentions in trivia and record books? Well, they also have the smallest average birth weight of babies in the United States, a natural altitude phenomenon not limited to the human species. If you visit from a much lower elevation, the beer is likely to get you drunk faster than back home and, because you're starved for oxygen, that headache might not be a hangover, but acute mountain sickness (AMS), caused by the altitude.

Take a walk around town, and check out America's Highest Everything. America's Highest Video Store (601 Harrison Ave.). America's Highest Chinese Restaurant (500 Harrison Ave.). America's Highest

Bowling Alley (1717 N. Poplar St.). America's Highest Laundromat (1707 N. Poplar St.). America's Highest Coffee House (711 Harrison Ave.). And don't forget America's Highest Pizza Hut (2017 N. Poplar St.).

Leadville Chamber of Commerce, 809 Harrison Ave., PO Box 861, Leadville, CO 80461

(800) 933-3901 or (719) 486-3900

E-mail: leadville@LeadvilleUSA.com

Hours: Always visible

Cost: Free

www.leadvilleusa.com

Directions: Along Rte. 24.

Horace, Augusta, and Baby Doe Tabor

Horace and Augusta Tabor moved to Oro City (later Leadville) in 1860 during the town's initial gold rush and set up a mercantile in California Gulch. Augusta, the first woman at the camp, was well-liked by the miners. She was also the first "banker" in the region, entrusted with their gold dust.

Miners at that time ran grubstake accounts where they offered creditors a stake in their finds. Horace bought a third of an unproductive mine for a "worthless" $17 grubstake; the Little Pittsburgh Mine turned out to be sitting on a rich silver vein, and Tabor was soon filthy rich.

Horace and Augusta lived at 312 Harrison Avenue from 1877 to 1881. Horace became the town's first postmaster, and first mayor in 1878. Their home was moved to 116 E. Fifth Street in 1879 where they entertained Ulysses S. Grant.

Tabor Cottage, 116 E. Fifth St., Leadville, CO 80461

(719) 486-0551

Hours: June–October, daily 9 A.M.–5 P.M.; November–May, Wednesday–Saturday
9 A.M.–5 P.M.

Cost: Free

Directions: One block east of Harrison Ave. on Fifth St.

Tabor used his proceeds from the Little Pittsburgh to buy the Matchless Mine for $117,000 in 1879. Shortly thereafter he left Augusta, the woman who had stood beside him from the beginning, for the younger and prettier Elizabeth McCourt Doe, better known as Baby Doe. Baby Doe was married at the time, and in a scheme to generate grounds for divorce,

refused to engage in sex with her husband, Harvey. He ran off to a Denver brothel (1943 Market St.) on March 2, 1880, not knowing he was being followed by one of Tabor's henchmen. Baby Doe had the goods on Harvey, and they were soon divorced.

The scandal shocked the nation. Despite this, Horace went on to become Colorado's lieutenant governor and later U.S. senator with a short 30-day appointment. Horace and Baby Doe were married in Washington, D.C., in 1883 in a ceremony attended by President Chester Arthur. Horace had the Tabor Opera House built for his beloved Baby Doe. Over the years, the stage would see the likes of Harry Houdini, John Philip Sousa's Marine Band, and Oscar Wilde.

Tabor Opera House, 308 Harrison Ave., Leadville, CO 80461

(719) 486-84091 or (303) 471-0984

E-mail: info@taboroperahouse.net

Hours: May–September, Sunday–Friday 9 A.M.–5:30 P.M.

Cost: Adults $4, Kids (5–12) $2

www.taboroperahouse.net

Directions: At the corner of Third St. and Harrison Ave.

OSCAR WILDE COMES TO TOWN

The Matchless Mine got a special visitor in 1882 when **Oscar Wilde** came to Leadville. Wilde was on a lecture and sightseeing tour of the West. While reading a passage from the *Autobiography of Benvenuto Cellini* for the Leadville miners, somebody asked why Benvenuto couldn't come to Leadville to read it himself. Wilde informed the audience that Cellini was dead, at which point the crowd asked, "Who shot him?" If Wilde needed any further evidence of frontier justice, he saw it at a local saloon: a sign over the bar read, "Please Do Not Shoot the Pianist. He Is Doing His Best."

To show their appreciation to the visiting playwright, the Matchless hosted a dinner for Wilde in the depths of the mine. He later described the three-course meal: "Having got into the heart of the mountain, I had supper, the first course being whiskey, the second whiskey, and the third whiskey."

Horace's bad advice.
Photo by author, courtesy of the Matchless Mine

All was going well until the Silver Panic of 1893 left Horace and Baby Doe bankrupt. Horace worked for some time on the patronage of old friends as Denver's postmaster. He died almost penniless on April 10, 1899, in room 302 of Denver's Winsor Hotel. His last words to Baby Doe were, "Hold on to the Matchless. It will make millions again!"

Hold on to it? She didn't even own it! Nevertheless, Baby Doe moved into a cabin over the Matchless Mine and the current owner didn't stop her; the hole had run dry years earlier, and he figured she was harmless. Baby Doe lived in the shack for another 36 years, always hoping for that elusive strike. She was found frozen to death on March 7, 1935, by deliveryman Elmer Kutzleb. She hadn't been seen since February 20. Her body was sprawled out in the shape of a cross on the cabin floor. Baby Doe was buried at Mt. Olivet Cemetery in Wheat Ridge (12801 W. 44th Ave., (303) 424-5263) next to Horace.

And what ever happened to Augusta? She took a $250,000 divorce settlement from Horace, parlayed it through shrewd investments into a half-million, and lived with the support and sympathy of her friends until her death in 1895. Not bad for a spurned woman.

Artifacts from the lives of Horace and Baby Doe are scattered around the state. The Frontier Historical Museum in Glenwood Springs (1001 Colorado Ave., (970) 945-4448) has their bed and a "crazy quilt" made from Baby Doe's elaborate wardrobe. Baby Doe's wedding dress, a solid silver invitation to the couple's wedding, and Horace's watch fob (found in the shack after Baby Doe's death) are in the collection of the Colorado History Museum in Denver (1300 Broadway, (303) 866-5736), and her piano is in Denver's Oxford Hotel (1600 Seventeenth St., (303) 628-5400).

Matchless Mine, 414 E. Seventh St., Leadville, CO 80461

(719) 486-0371

Hours: June–August, daily 9 A.M.–5 P.M.

Cost: Adults $3.50, Kids $1

www.matchlessmine.com

Directions: Two miles east of town on Seventh St.

LEADVILLE
"Leadville has 10 months of winter and two months of late fall."
—Doc Holliday

Jesse James reportedly buried $50,000 in stolen gold and silver in Half Moon Gulch, two miles south of Leadville.

To stay in form, Leadville throws a St. Patrick's Day Practice Parade on the Saturday closest to September 17 (six months ahead of the actual St. Patrick's Day) each year.

For a bull to walk on a Leadville street, it must wear a bell, whistle, horn, headlight, or taillight.

The Ice Palace Has Melted

People who live in glass houses shouldn't throw stones, and people who live in ice houses should pray for cold weather. That seems to be the lesson of Leadville's Ice Palace of 1896.

Leadville's economic boom years were long gone by 1895 when town boosters came up with the idea of a winter carnival. The Crystal Carnival Association's plan was to attract tourists to their mountaintop village, thereby keeping Leadville from becoming a ghost town.

First, the centerpiece, a 320-by-450-foot Ice Palace with two nine-story octagonal towers, constructed with 5,000 tons of ice over 36 days by 300 previously unemployed miners. Steel and wooden timbers formed the framework, but were hidden by ice block columns. The palace had an skating rink in its center, flanked on both sides by two heated ballrooms. One, decorated in pre-Broncos orange and blue, was a restaurant. The other was used for dances, many of them featuring the Fort Dodge Cowboy Band. Colored lights glowed from within the frozen walls, giving it an otherworldly appearance at night.

Flowers, fruit, and bottles of beer were also frozen into the Ice Palace's walls, and the structure was filled, and surrounded, with stuffed Colorado wildlife and ice sculptures of prospectors, burros, and Lady Leadville, a 19-foot maiden pointing to the hills and the mines that made it all possible.

The carnival opened on January 1, 1896. (It would have opened on Christmas Day, but warm December weather had been melting the walls.) Adult admission was 50¢; kids got in for a quarter. Organizers hoped it would draw additional business for the town's hotels, restaurants, and saloons. However, because the train ride from Denver took nine hours *each way*, most visitors rode up, looked around, and headed back down the mountain. The Crystal Carnival was a financial disaster.

Unexpected chinook winds in March sent the palace to an early puddle. It closed for good on March 28. Earlier talk of rebuilding the Ice Palace year after year was quickly forgotten, and the frame structure was torn down. All that remains of the Ice Palace today is a building constructed with some of the leftover timbers. Today, it is a bed-and-breakfast. You can find a scale model of the Ice Palace at the National Mining Hall of Fame and Museum.

400–500 W. Seventh St., Leadville, CO 80461

No phone

Hours: Melted

Cost: Free

Directions: Between 6th and 8th Sts. on Capitol Hill.

Ice Palace Inn, 813 Spruce St., Leadville, CO 80461

(800) 754-2840 or (719) 486-8272

E-mail: ipalace@bwn.net

Hours: Open year-round

Cost: $89–$139/night

www.icepalaceinn.com

Directions: One block west of Harrison Ave., between 8th and 9th Sts.

Michelange-no

Father George M. Trunk was a doer, not a talker, so when he was assigned to the drab parish of St. Joseph's on August 1, 1924, he decided to spruce the place up. A fire had leveled the congregation's first chapel a year earlier, and the paint was still fresh on the replacement. To Trunk's eyes, which had recently caught a glimpse of the Sistine Chapel, there wasn't nearly enough paint on the ceiling.

Though not a trained artist, the 62-year-old pastor began painting his own murals on the St. Joseph's ceiling. And the walls. And the vestibule. And the Stations of the Cross. The large works have an almost impressionist feel, with blurry, pointillist pastels, but his Stations of the Cross more closely resemble icons of his native Slovenia. Though crude and somewhat disproportionate, the works reflect the determination of a can-do spirit.

St. Joseph's Church, Maple & Second Sts., Leadville, CO 80461

(719) 486-1591

Hours: Call ahead

Cost: Free

Directions: At the corner of Maple and W. Second Sts., four blocks west of Harrison Ave. (Rte. 24).

NEDERLAND

Fred, the former Nederland town cat, is buried on the town hall lawn.

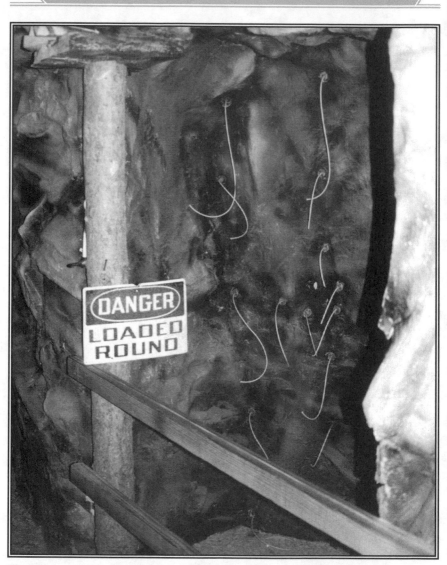

When they say, "No Smoking" in the museum, they mean *"NO SMOKING!"*
Photo by author, courtesy of the National Mining Hall of Fame and Museum

National Mining Hall of Fame and Museum

Mining. Most people don't think about how it affects their lives, but consider this: each American uses 40,000 pounds of mined material *each year*. That's just one of the eye-opening facts you'll learn in this corporate-sponsored museum. Located in a converted 100-year-old school, this museum chronicles this broad industry, from precious metals to coal to uranium, and unlike those dirty mine tours, there's no hard hat required here.

Check out the 23-ounce nugget from the Little Jonny Mine in the Gold Rush Room, along with rare samples of crystallized gold from far-away Siberia. Trace the development of mining through detailed dioramas. Step into the museum's two life-size replicas, a coal mine (circa 1900) with an underground mule pulling a cart, and a turn-of-the-century hard-rock mine with mannequins of a blacksmith, jackleg operator, assayer, hoist operator, and miner being lowered down a shaft in a cage. And the gift shop is crammed full of all your rock and mineral needs.

120 W. 9th St., PO Box 981, Leadville, CO 80461

(719) 486-1229

E-mail: nationalminingmuseum@bemail.com

Hours: May–October, daily 9 A.M.–5 P.M.; November–April, Monday–Friday 9 A.M.–3 P.M.

Cost: Adults $4, Seniors (62+) $3.50, Kids (6–11) $2

www.leadville.com/miningmuseum

Directions: One block west of Harrison Ave. (Rte. 24) on 9th St.

Manassa
Jack Dempsey Museum

Boxer Jack Dempsey was born in Manassa on June 24, 1895, to a schoolteacher and his wife. He soon gained a reputation as a no-holds-barred brawler, willing to punch out anyone's lights, even when very little money was at stake.

Dempsey fought his first "official" bout at the Moose Lodge in Montrose during the 1912 County Fair. His opponent was Fred Wood, the Fighting Blacksmith; Dempsey boxed under the nickname Kid Blackie, later changed to the Manassa Mauler. Dempsey knocked out Wood.

Dempsey worked at a series of Colorado mining camps, taking day jobs when he didn't have a fight lined up. He was a bouncer at the Pick 'n' Gad brothel (on Spruce Street) in Telluride, and washed dishes at the Senate, another whorehouse. He also spent time in Cripple Creek.

He became a national boxing legend after he won the World Title from Jess Willard in 1919, and remained the top draw in boxing for the next eight years. His 1923 bout with Frenchman Georges Carpentier was the first $1 million fight in history.

Dempsey retired in 1927 after losing to Gene Tunny during the infamous "Long Count" Battle at Chicago's Soldier Field. Following a short career as a movie star, he moved to New York and opened a restaurant. He died in 1983.

The folks in Manassa have never forgotten their hometown bully, and have opened a museum in his birthplace. The family didn't stay there all that long, but Jack's fists made a lasting impression—mostly on other people's faces.

Jack Dempsey Museum, 412 Main St., Manassa, CO 81141

(719) 843-5207

Hours: June–September, Monday–Saturday 9 A.M.–5 P.M.

Cost: Free

www.cmgww.com/sports/dempsey/index.html

Directions: Between 4th and 5th Sts., on Rte. 142 (Main St.).

Holy hillside!
Photo courtesy of the Colorado Historical Society, WHJ-2399

Minturn and Salida
Holy Hills

The Colorado Rockies are, without a doubt, majestic. But could they also be holy?

Take the 14,005-foot Mount of the Holy Cross, 10 miles southwest of Minturn. From mid- to late summer, snow accumulated in three large ravines forms a bright white cross—1,500 feet from top to bottom, against the blue-gray mountaintop. Water from when this holy snow melts runs down the central ravine and collects in a small pool called Bowl of Tears. Some believe that handkerchiefs dipped in this water will absorb healing powers, and for years pastors and priests would bring pack-mule trains up the hill for this purpose.

Others have not been content to receive secondhand healings. In 1928, a crippled woman was carried to the top of Notch Mountain and, after gazing at the cross, was able to walk back down under her own power. Or so the story goes.

Sadly, recent rock slides have obscured the right arm of the once clear image. Were the avalanches the result of typical geologic erosion, or were they a sign from the heavens to a sinful nation? The debate rages on.

Mount of the Holy Cross, Holy Cross Wilderness Area, White River National Forest, 24747 U.S. Highway 24, PO Box 190, Minturn, CO 81645

(970) 827-5715 or (970) 827-9343

Hours: Daylight, summer (July is best)

Cost: Free

www.fs.fed.us/r2/whiteriver/

Directions: Best viewed from atop Notch Mountain, just east of the cross.

Each summer another mountain, south of the Mount of the Holy Cross, is the site of a fleeting apparition. During a couple of days each June, on the eastern face of Mount Shavano, the image of an angel appears in the melting snow. It is hundreds of feet tall and can be seen for miles around. Its arms outstretched, its head cocked slightly to the right, the Angel of Shavano beams its blessings down upon the good folk of Salida, 14 miles to the southeast. And then, under the punishing rays of the high-altitude sun, it disappears for another year.

Nonbelievers say the Angel of Shavano looks more like E.T. It's hard to argue.

Mount Shavano, San Isabel National Forest, Salida, CO 81201

(719) 539-3591

Hours: Daylight, June

Cost: Free

www.fs.fed.us/r2/psicc/sanisabel.htm

Directions: Look northwest from Salida, on the eastern face of the mountain.

Who needs a back seat?
Photo courtesy of Best Western's Movie Manor

Monte Vista
Movie Manor

It gets rather cold at night in this part of the state, even in the summer, a factor that limits the usefulness of a drive-in theater. But if that theater was bordered by a comfy motel, with each room's window pointing toward the screen—now that's a great idea!

Movie Manor was born out of just that type of thinking. George and Edna Kelloff built their motel adjacent to the Star Drive-In in 1955. The motel has 54 rooms, most named after a film star of yesteryear. Today, Movie Manor is part of the Best Western chain.

Before the movie starts, why not have a bite at the motel's Academy Awards Restaurant with its displaced Hollywood theme? Check out the handprints in cement. Movie stars? No, mostly Kelloff family members. Save room for popcorn and candy, which you can pick up at the snack bar in the lobby. Head back to your room where the sound is piped in from the film projected on the outside screen. The Star Drive-In does get

traditional car-bound customers, but they must make do in cramped back seats, whereas lodgers can make out on queen- and king-size beds.

Best Western's Movie Manor, 2830 W. Rte. 160, Monte Vista, CO 81144

(800) 771-9468 or (719) 852-5921

Hours: Call ahead; movies shown May–September only

Cost: $50/night

www.coloradovacation.com/motel/movie

Directions: Two and a half miles west of town on Rte. 160.

You're not in the Everglades anymore.
Photo by author, courtesy of the Colorado Alligator Farm

Mosca
Colorado Alligator Farm

Gators . . . in the *mountains*? Hard to believe, but it's true—at least on the Colorado Alligator Farm it is! As you might suspect, these reptiles are not indigenous to the region but are recent imports. This operation was started as a fish farm in 1987 by Edwin and Lynne Young. Situated on a natural hot spring that supplies 87-degree water all year round, the farm was even more successful than the couple had hoped. The fish population was exploding, so alligators were imported to dispose of the dead and excess fish.

But the Colorado Alligator Farm is more than just a fish- and gator-breeding operation. They've got a tank full of sharks, other reptiles in pens, a picnic area, and a gift shop that sells fresh alligator meat. Twice a day, at noon and 4 P.M., you're invited to watch a feeding and wrestling demonstration inside the chain-link pen. If you're lucky, they'll bring out Zebulon, the only live alligator ever to make it to the top of Pikes Peak (with a little help from his human handlers).

The best time to visit the farm is in early August for the annual Gatorfest, the state's one and only Gator Rodeo! There are many events throughout the day, but the best is when six brave but dopey contestants compete to rope and wrangle the biggest gators in the ponds. Whoever comes up with the heaviest reptile, without losing a hand, foot, or worse, is the champion.

9162 County Road 9 North, Mosca, CO 81146

(719) 378-2612

E-mail: lynne@gatorfarm.com

Hours: June-August, daily 9 A.M.–7 P.M.; September–May, daily 9 A.M.–5 P.M.

Cost: Adults $5, Kids (6–12) $2.50

www.gatorfarm.com

Directions: Seventeen miles north of Alamosa on Rte. 17.

Great Sand Dunes National Park

Nobody has yet fully explained why the Great Sand Dunes are where they are. It's perhaps too convenient to say that the 750-foot sand peaks that cover 40 square miles (10 miles long, 4 miles deep) of the northeast corner of the San Luis Valley were blown in from across this desert-like region, but the chemical composition of the sand granules doesn't quite match that of the rest of the valley. Also, why aren't there sand dunes in the downwind corners of every valley on the face of the earth? Nope, something funny is *definitely* going on here.

Could the dunes be, as some paranormal zealots have suggested, the doorway to the Underworld? With the region's never-ceasing tales of UFOs, some find this theory even more believable. Also, what about those every-so-often reports of web-footed horses that live on the dunes?

Even if you don't see any aliens or duck-footed ponies, this park is worth the drive. The Great Sand Dunes is one of this country's least utilized and most beautiful national parks, and because of its remote location, you won't get tied up in a camper traffic jam just trying to get in.

11500 Highway 150, Mosca, CO 81146

(719) 378-2312

Hours: Visitors Center, 9:30 A.M.–4:30 P.M. (6 P.M. June–September); Park always open

Cost: Adults (over 17) $3, Kids Free

www.nps.gov/grsa

Directions: Fourteen miles east of Alamosa on Rte. 160, then 20 miles north on Rte. 150.

Ladies and gentlemen—Grandpa on Ice!

Nederland
Grandpa's in the Tuff Shed

Even measured against Nederland standards, Trygve Bauge was a little odd. It wasn't just that the Norwegian hippie founded the Boulder Polar Bear Club where he and his friends would jump into icy Wonderland Lake every New Year's Day. Nor was it the "disaster-proof" castle he built overlooking the town. Even the run-in with security at Stapleton Airport—he tested the boundaries of free speech by demanding the right to tell a hijacking joke to a ticket agent—seemed tame compared to what would soon be learned about the contents of his backyard shed.

As a result of the airport joke incident, INS agents sought and succeeded in getting the immigrant deported in 1994. Trygve's mother, Aud (pronounced "odd"), revealed to a local reporter that her son still had two frozen bodies in the shed behind his castle. Police searched the property and found two cryogenically preserved corpses. One, Al Campbell, was wrapped in a sleeping bag; his family was contacted and his thawing body was returned to Chicago for burial. The other turned out to be Bredo Morstoel, Trygve's grandpa who'd died in Norway in 1982.

Though they were on shaky legal ground, town officials wanted Morstoel's body removed, buried, or both, but Aud put up a fight. By the time the council could convene a hearing, the Nederland community had grown attached to their Grandpopsicle. Though Aud returned to Norway to be with Trygve, Grandpa Bredo has been preserved thanks to the generous efforts of local folk, namely Bo Shaffer who delivers dry ice to the Tuff Shed every three weeks.

A movie about the strange sequence of events was filmed by Robin and Kathy Beeck, and won the 1998 Phillip Lloyd Prize at the Telluride Mountainfilm Festival. You can still see the shed today, but Grandpa doesn't say much.

Alpine Dr., Nederland, CO 80466

No phone

Hours: Always visible

Cost: Free

Directions: Head east on Big Springs Dr. (just south of the grocery store) until it meets with Alpine Dr., then look up the hill for the castle.

NEDERLAND
Nederland calls itself the Small Town with the Big Heart.

Where does a 10-ton grandma sit?

Penrose
World's Largest Rocking Chair

Where does a 10-ton grandma sit? Anywhere she wants! Chances are, if she knew about it, she would want to sit on the 9,100-pound rocking chair outside a Penrose fruit stand. While the woodwork isn't polished and detailed—more Paul Bunyan than Ethan Allen—it still has a certain rustic charm.

The rocking chair was built in 1990 by Doxey's Apple Shed as a promotional gimmick; and it is one of a kind. The chair is 21 feet high,

14 feet wide, and pieced together out of hand-hewn Douglas fir trunks. Some killjoy has put stops under the rockers, so even if you do crawl up to the seat for an Edith Ann pose, you won't be able to tip it back and forth. And thath the truth—thffffttt!

Doxey's Apple Shed, F St., Penrose, CO 81240

No phone

Hours: Always visible

Cost: Free

Directions: At the north end of town on F St. (Rte. 115).

PAGOSA SPRINGS

Myrtle Snow of Pagosa Springs claims to have seen five baby dinosaurs near town when she was three years old. A few months after her May 1935 sighting, a neighboring farmer shot a scaly beast when it attacked his cattle.

More than $5 million in gold bars is rumored to be buried on Treasure Mountain near Pagosa Springs, just east of the Wolf Creek Pass summit.

PONCHA SPRINGS

Billy the Kid and **Jesse James** have both spent the night at the Jackson Hotel in Poncha Springs.

SAN LUIS

Established on April 5, 1851, San Luis is Colorado's oldest town.

TWIN LAKES

Twin Lakes holds an annual Tomato War in late summer to dispose of its excess tomatoes.

Rye
Bishop Castle

When you see Bishop Castle for the first time, it's hard to believe that it has been built single-handedly. But Jim Bishop has been at it for more than 30 years, and isn't anywhere near done. But, as they say, great works of art are never completed, just abandoned. As it stands now, Bishop has already broken the record for the World Largest Structure Built by a Single Person.

Bishop first purchased this land for $450 at the age of 15 using money he had saved mowing lawns. He dropped out of high school in the 11th grade after seeing a trunkload of chickens that the football team had dyed the school's colors for a pep rally. He felt that if that's what school was all about, he wanted no part of it.

Bishop began building his castle in 1969 using rocks collected from the San Isabel National Forest. That's where he started getting into trouble. The Forest Service wanted Jim to pay $16 per ton, and until he did, they refused to acknowledge his presence with a road sign or mention in any promotional literature for travelers in this region. (Things were eventually settled.)

Never mind those bureaucrats; Bishop knew that word would get around. And it did. The castle will have three 160-foot towers when finished, as well as a great hall, torture chamber (federal agents beware!), scenic elevators powered by the sun, waterfalls, and an astronomical observatory. He's already installed the fire-breathing dragon made of old stainless steel hospital trays. When he's done, he hopes to erect another castle for his very understanding wife.

The best part about Bishop's Castle is that it's wide open to the public, so long as you sign the accident waiver before entering. The sturdy structure is filled with creepy winding staircases, half-finished balconies, children running everywhere, and parents standing down on the ground screaming, "Harrison! Brittney! I told you—*NO HIGHER! GET DOWN FROM THERE!*"

Route 165, Rye, CO 81069
Contact: 1529 Claremont Ave., Pueblo, CO 81004
(719) 564-4366 or (719) 485-3040
Hours: May–September, daily 9 A.M.–7 P.M. (but call ahead)

Cost: Free

www.bishopcastle.org or www.castlecollectables.com

Directions: On Rte. 165, 24 miles east of I-25, north of the intersection with Rte. 78 from Beulah.

Salida
E.T.'s Landing

Something BIG visited this little town on August 27, 1995, and Brandy Edwards was the first to see it. This six-year-old spotted a triangular object hovering near town, and she told her father about it. Many parents might ignore their child or chalk such reports up to an over-active imagination. Not Tim Edwards. He went to see what his daughter was talking about, and sure enough, there was something "dancing" around the sun's rays.

Edwards videotaped more than six minutes of the craft's activity; he was the only person of the 23 witnesses that day to do so. UFOlogists claim it is one of the best pieces of extraterrestrial evidence ever documented, while others dismiss it as an optical illusion. Will anyone ever know? Edwards has rolled out the welcome mat in Salida, changing the name of his restaurant from the Patio Pancake to E.T.'s Landing. The menu is primarily burgers and Mexican dishes—no Martian munchies yet—but they have decorated the walls with photographs of flying saucers and images from NASA's Hubble telescope.

1015 E. Highway 50, Salida, CO 81201

(719) 539-1519

Hours: Wednesday–Monday 11 A.M.–9 P.M.

Cost: Meals $6–$12

Directions: Three blocks west of the intersection of Rtes. 291 and 50.

San Luis
The Penitentes

The Brothers of Light, better known as the Penitentes, are a vanishing breed. It's not hard to understand why they have trouble finding converts. This Catholic lay society has been operating in the San Luis Valley region since 1599, and has a strong focus on the sacrament of penance. No Our Father's and Hail Mary's for them—but how about a healthy dose of self-flagellation? At one time, it was not uncommon to see a line of Penitentes beating themselves with whips until they drew blood, standing on cacti, or walking around with stones in their shoes, all in an attempt to expiate sin. And during Lent, one lucky fellow would be chosen to drag a wooden cross to a mountaintop where he would be hung up for the afternoon.

Well, most of the rough stuff is in the past—at least as far as outsiders are concerned. Today, followers still have Good Friday processions, but they're less physically abusive. Instead, they sing sorrowful folk songs called *alabados*, or songs of praise. You'll learn more at a local museum, which is a replica of a *morada* chapel used by the Penitentes of the Hermandad.

While in San Luis, don't pass up the opportunity to see the town's famous station of the cross statues. Each of the 15 stations has been re-created with full-size bronze statues for the full effect. Sculptor Huberto Maestras used local folk for models, so don't be surprised if you recognize the faces of the Roman guards and weeping women at the nearby Dairy Queen.

San Luis Museum and Cultural Center, 401 Church Pl., PO Box 657, San Luis, CO 81152
(719) 672-3611
Hours: June–September, daily 10 A.M.–4 P.M.; October–May, Monday–Friday 10 A.M.–4 P.M.
Cost: Adults $1, Kids (5–12) 50¢
Directions: Just east of Rte. 159 (Main St.) on Church Pl.
Stations of the Cross, Sangre de Cristo Parish, PO Box 326, San Luis, CO 81152
(719) 672-3685
Hours: Always visible
Cost: Free
Directions: On the north side of Rte. 142, just west of the Rte. 159 (Main St.) intersection.

VAIL
The Colorado Ski Museum and Ski Hall of Fame is located in the heart of Vail (231 S. Frontage Rd., (970) 476-1876).

Silver Cliff
Ghost Light in the Cemetery

Ghost stories of floating blue lights in abandoned cemeteries are not uncommon—they're often perpetuated by Boy Scout troop leaders and drunken high school partiers as a means of frightening others. But the ghost lights at the Silver Cliff Cemetery have been spotted since 1882, long before the Boy Scouts and local secondary education. Old as they are, they can't be dismissed as reflections of electric lights or automobiles.

The Silver Cliff ghost lights have been given a sort of legitimacy by virtue of being mentioned in both the *New York Times* and *National Geographic*. They're said to be the size of a basketball, hover in the air at about knee level, and appear most often on overcast evenings. They've been spotted most often near the Becker and Schmitt headstones. Are they the disturbed energy of native spirits? Or miners' lights from long-dead diggers? Nobody seems to know for sure.

Silver Cliff Cemetery, Mill St., Silver Cliff, CO 81252

No phone

Hours: At night

Cost: Free

Directions: One mile south of Main St. (Rte. 96) on Mill St.

VICTOR

Radio broadcaster **Lowell Thomas** grew up in Victor. His childhood home is now a museum (Victor Ave. & 3rd St.).

Vice presidential candidate **Teddy Roosevelt** was assaulted with a banner pole at a Victor campaign rally in September 1900.

WINTER PARK

Winter Park claims to be the Powder Snow Capital of the World.

Silver Plume
Griffin's Ghost

Nobody quite knew what to make of a young miner named Clifford Griffin. He was quiet, prosperous, and didn't frequent the saloons or whorehouses. What's more, he was British, and he played a violin. But he had fled his homeland after his fiancée was found murdered the night before their wedding, and that sounded downright suspicious.

The woman's killer was never apprehended, and Griffin wouldn't speak about the tragic event with his new neighbors. Did he have something to hide? Whatever the case, he was a sad fellow and spent much of his free time sitting on his cabin porch, high over town near his mine, scraping out mournful tunes.

Folks listened to Griffin's nightly concerts until June 19, 1887, when, after his last song, he shot himself in the heart and tumbled into a grave he had dug for himself. Locals covered him up and erected a granite marker, but that didn't fully put him to rest. His spirit is still said to wander the town playing the violin.

All Around Town, Silver Plume, CO 80444

No phone

Hours: Evenings, mostly

Cost: Free

Directions: In the hills around town.

Steamboat Springs
Slipping and Sliding

You have to have at least some level of competency in winter driving to enroll at the Bridgestone Winter Driving School. To get to the school in the first place you have to make your way up to Steamboat Springs in the middle of winter over some potentially treacherous mountain passes. Hopefully, by the time you graduate, you're much better prepared to head back down from the mountains.

Though you probably heard it a thousand times in driver's ed, "When you start to slide, take your foot off the gas and turn your steering wheel in the direction you wish to go." This response comes easier without all the nervous energy generated by the possibility of sideswiping a busload of skiers. At this unique (and totally rad!) school, you're trained on a closed course where you'll get plenty of practice skidding around without hitting anyone. After they certify you, look out ice and snow! No chain law is going to frighten you away—even if it should.

The Bridgestone Winter Driving School, PO Box 774167, 1850 Ski Times Square Dr., Steamboat Springs, CO 80477

(800) WHY-SKID or (970) 879-6104

E-mail: mail@winterdrive.com

Hours: December–March, by appointment

Cost: $145–$1,475

www.winterdrive.com

Directions: Take Mt. Werner Rd. east off Rte. 40; the school is off Mt. Werner Circle.

Vail
Captain Craig Button's Wild Ride

Given recent American events, the April 2, 1997, crash of Captain Craig Button's A-10 Thunderbolt II into a Colorado mountain seems all the more unsettling. Button was based at Davis–Monthan Air Force Base in Tucson, Arizona, and during a routine training session, he veered away from his flight formation and headed north.

After an 800-mile journey, he crashed his $8.8 million jet near Vail. It took recovery teams almost three weeks before they found the plane on the side of Gold Dust Peak. When the Air Force finally dug out the wreckage in the early summer, they discovered that the plane's four 500-pound bombs were missing. Uh-oh. Hikers in the Holy Cross Wilderness Area will notice signs on how to recognize a bomb if they find one—as if that would be difficult: squirrel . . . pine tree . . . quarter-ton bomb . . . OK, got it!

And why did Button do it? Early unsubstantiated rumors swirled that he was soon to be outed as gay by another Davis–Monthan pilot, and was distressed about the idea of being discharged from the Air Force. A later theory, advanced by the Air Force in a "psychological autopsy," claimed Button had been dumped by his girlfriend and shunned by his pacifist mother who was unhappy with his career choice. His mother denied this, and her story is certainly believable—she is *married* to an Air Force pilot. Some UFO nuts think Button was actually *abducted* and is now working on an alien mother ship called Tagamont. But the truth is, nobody but Craig Button knows for sure, and he ain't talking.

Gold Dust Peak, Holy Cross Wilderness, Vail, CO 81657

Contact: White River National Forest, 24747 U.S. Highway 24, PO Box 190, Minturn, CO 81645

No phone

Hours: Always visible

Cost: Free

www.fs.fcd.us/r2/whiteriver/

Directions: Fifteen miles southwest of Vail.

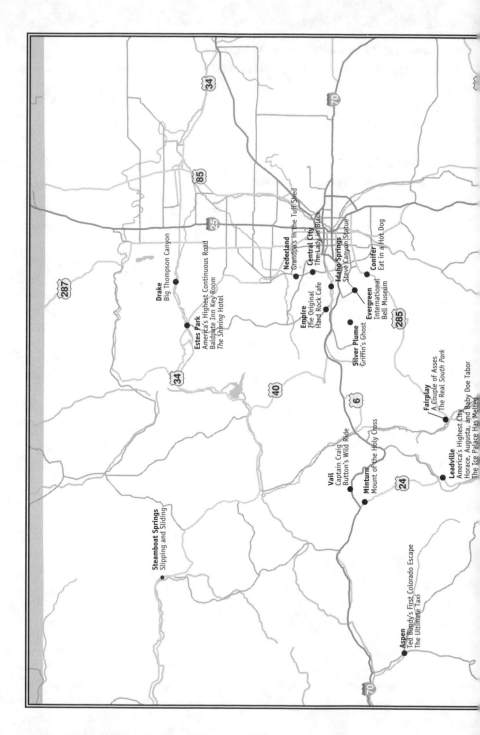

Drake
Big Thompson Canyon

Estes Park
America's Highest Continuous Road
Baldpate Inn Key Room
The Shining Hotel

Nederland
Grandpa's in the Tuff Shed

Central City
The Lady in Black

Idaho Springs
Steve Canyon Statue

Conifer
Eat in a Hot Dog

Empire
The Original
Hard Rock Cafe

Evergreen
International
Bell Museum

Silver Plume
Griffin's Ghost

Fairplay
A Couple of Asses
The Real *South Park*

Leadville
America's Highest City
Horace, Augusta, and Baby Doe Tabor
The Ice Palace Has Melted

Vail
Captain Craig
Button's Wild Ride

Minturn
Mount of the Holy Cross

Steamboat Springs
Slipping and Sliding

Aspen
Ted Bundy's First Colorado Escape
The Ultimate Taxi

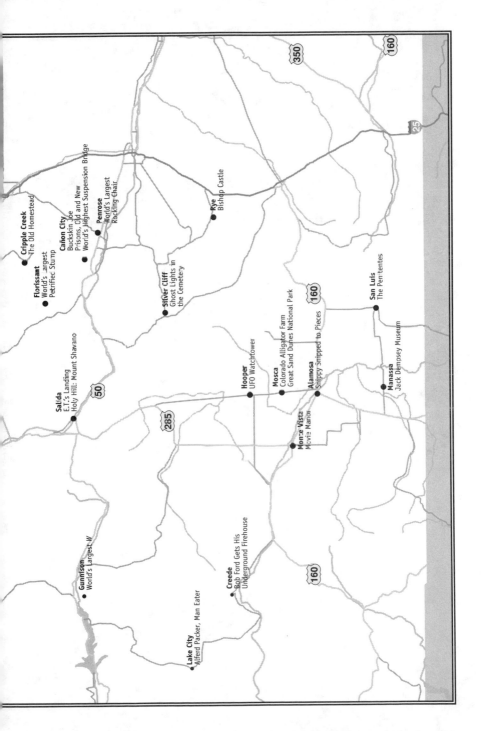

5

THE WESTERN SLOPE

Some Colorado tourists subscribe to a Denvercentric or Aspencentric view of the state, and yes, it is sometimes hard to remember that there are places to visit on the other side of the Continental Divide. But if you willingly ignore all that the western slope has to offer, you're going to miss out on a whole lot of weirdness.

Where else in the state will you find an annual festival to honor a headless chicken? The front range brags that it has Buffalo Bill's body (though some say they stole it from Cody, Wyoming); but Glenwood Springs has the remains of gun-slingers Doc Holliday and Kid Curry. And only on the western slope can you see 10-story beaver dams, arrows made from telephone poles, and the blue highways driven by Thelma and Louise.

What's more, the laid-back attitude of the western slope can't be beat. Who's got the World's Largest Outdoor Hot Springs? They do! And while people in Denver were using their creative energy to invent and refine the evil Denver Boot, some enter-prising maids in Glenwood Springs gave birth to the world's first cuddly teddy bear. That's something to be proud of.

So hop in that car and drive, drive, drive (it'll take you a while to get there) to the wonderful western slope—you'll be awfully glad you did!

Cortez
Four Corners

Four Corners, the way-out-of-the-way intersection of Colorado, New Mexico, Arizona, and Utah, is special in that it is the only spot where four states meet in the United States. Big deal, you say? Well, this geographic oddity offers you the unique opportunity to be in four different states *at the same time!* Think of it as a game of cartographic Twister: place one hand or foot in each of the states, and your belly button will hang just over the point where they meet.

This amazing site is made possible by a jog in Colorado's western boundary during its initial platting. On most Colorado maps, if you follow the western border near the town of Bedrock in Montrose County, you'll see it make a one-minute deviation eastward, allowing the Utah–Colorado boundary to run directly into the Arizona–New Mexico line. Had surveyors not done this, the intersection would have been a mile off.

Four Corners is managed by the Navajo Nation, and is surrounded by many trinket-filled souvenir huts (though fewer than there used to be after a 1996 fire). Before making the looooong trip, atheists take note: "Here Meet, Under God, Four States" is engraved on the simple cement platform.

Contact: Navajo Parks and Recreation Department, PO Box 9000, Window Rock, AZ
   86515
(928) 871-6647
Hours: May–August, daily 7 A.M.–7 P.M.; September–April, daily 8 A.M.–5 P.M.
Cost: Adults $2.50
www.navajonation.parks.org/fourcorners.html
Directions: Twenty miles south of Cortez on Rte. 666/160, 18 miles west on Rte. 160, and 100 yards off the road.

BAYFIELD

John "Mickey" Craig, who once owned the Wilderness Trails Dude Ranch north of Bayfield, was active in state GOP politics and played a bit part in the film *Butch Cassidy and the Sundance Kid*. He was also one of the Heaven's Gate cult members who committed suicide in Rancho Santa Fe, California, in 1997.

Mesa Verde National Park

The Anasazi ruins of southwest Colorado are home to some of the most recognizable archeological remnants of pre-Columbian America. And along with caravans of tourists, they've attracted a cottage industry of conflicting theories as to what they suggest about the early history of the region.

The official story goes something like this: The Anasazi (meaning "the ancient ones") moved into this area in third century B.C. They built cliff dwellings as a way of protecting themselves from the elements and providing security from critters and hostile neighbors. There are dozens of cliff dwellings, not all of which are open to the public, but Cliff House is the most elaborate. Cliff House was abandoned by the late 13th century after a 24-year drought. Where did the Anasazi go when they left Mesa Verde? Some say they traveled south—and that the Aztecs were their descendants.

That's interesting, but where did the Anasazi originally come from? New Age author Jean Hunt has a theory: the Anasazi were the descendants of the lost continent of Atlantis! Why? Some unearthed skeletons indicate the inhabitants had dolichocephalic (long) skulls, a physical trait common in the ancient Mediterranean, where Atlantis was last seen. Also, a sunflower-shaped sculpture carved entirely through water erosion and discovered near Mesa Verde raised Hunt's suspicions. Clearly this was the art of the Atlantean culture. OK . . . whatever . . .

Another mystery arose several years ago when stone scrape marks were found on other unearthed human bones dating to A.D. 1150. Scientists suggested that cannibalism might have been practiced here. Others claimed the evidence pointed to a ritual sacrifice of those suspected of witchcraft—but nobody was *eaten*.

Mesa Verde National Park, PO Box 8, Mesa Verde National Park, CO 81330

(970) 529-4465 or (970) 529-4461

Hours: Daily 8 A.M.–5 P.M. (6:30 P.M. in summer)

Cost: $10/car

www.nps.gov/meve

Directions: South off Rte. 160, 10 miles east of Cortez.

Anasazi Heritage Center, 27501 Colorado Rte. 184, Dolores, CO 81323

(970) 882-4811

E-mail: meastin@co.blm.gov

Hours: March–October, daily 9 A.M.–5 P.M.; November–February, daily 9 A.M.–4 P.M.

Cost: Adults $3, Kids (under 18) free

www.co.blm.gov/ahc/hmepge.htm

Directions: Three miles west of town on Rte. 184.

Delta
Charles Kuralt, Accomplice to Herbicide

It stood beside Route 50 for years, a lone piñon pine atop Fools' Hill northwest of Delta on the road to Grand Junction. Local elves began hanging ornaments and garlands on the tree around the holidays, and a quaint tradition was born. Then Charles Kuralt opened his big mouth.

After the tree appeared in a segment of *On the Road*, more and more people visited it to leave an ornament. One visitor decided to decorate it with a string of lights powered by a car battery. The warmth of the bulbs dried out the needles; the tree withered and died. The only adult pine tree for miles around, and Kuralt had to point it out to some bumbling, decorating killer. Good going, Chuck, you blockhead.

Well, some good soul has planted a new tree atop Fools' Hill. Hopefully, people will show some restraint this time. That means you, dear reader!

Fools' Hill, Rte. 50, Delta, CO 81416

No phone

Hours: Always visible

Cost: Free

Directions: Fifteen miles west of town.

Dinosaur
Dinosaur National Monument

"Hop aboard!" the tram guide tells you. "It's just a short trip to the dinosaur quarry!" You're quite aware of how this story will likely play out: a genetically engineered Jurassic creature will attack the shuttle, eating arrogant lawyers, money-grubbing theme-park creators, and chubby, unattractive paleontologists. Hop aboard? No, thank you!

Well, there's no need to be worried at Dinosaur National Monument. If these folks tried to resurrect giant species, they'd have a lot of work ahead of them. First of all, the fossils uncovered at this quarry are still tangled like a pile of Pick-Up Sticks. Though the first apatosaurus/ brontosaurus and brachiosaurus skeletons ever discovered were pulled from this fossil bed, current specimens are not removed from the giant rock wall but studied *in situ*. It's the world's oldest jigsaw puzzle.

Because the monument straddles the Colorado–Utah border, each state has its own visitor's center. Though the majority of the monument lies in Colorado, the main quarry is in Utah.

Visitors Center, 4545 E. Highway 40, Dinosaur, CO 81610
(970) 374-3000
E-mail: DINO_Superintendent@nps.gov
Hours: June–August, daily 8 A.M.–6 P.M.; September–May, daily Monday–Friday
   8 A.M.–4:30 P.M.
Cost: $10/car
www.nps.gov/dino/
Directions: Two miles east of town on Rte. 40.

Dinosaur Quarry, PO Box 128, Jensen, UT 84035
(435) 789-2115
Hours: Daily 8 A.M.–4:30 P.M.
Cost: Included in admission to the park
Directions: Seven miles north of Jensen.

CATTLE CREEK
Married couples may not have sex in "any lake, river, or stream" in Cattle Creek.

CRAIG
Craig hosts a Wild Game & Roadkill Cookoff at its Grand Olde West Days each Memorial Day.

Richard Barker, a child performer who was the inspiration for **Buster Brown**, moved to Craig after serving in the army during World War I. He lived on a ranch outside of town until his death in 1976.

It's fueled by old dinosaurs.

Dinosaur Town

It's tough to fight City Hall, particularly when it's guarded by a stegosaurus. But don't be afraid—it's just a concrete statue. This town (called Artesia until 1965) has several cement dinosaurs scattered

around, including a triceratops at the intersection of routes 40 and 64. Its few streets are named after well-known species: Tyrannosaurus Trail, Brachiosaurus Boulevard, Plateosaurus Place, Triceratops Terrace, Androdemus Alley, and Stegosaurus Freeway (where the Dino-Bone Rock Shop is located).

The best dinosaur in town guards a junkyard just east of the Conoco station. Made from old oil drums that once contained the petrochemical remains of these prehistoric creatures, it's the world's nastiest junkyard dog.

Dinosaur Area Chamber of Commerce, PO Box 202, Dinosaur, CO 81610

(800) 864-4405

Hours: Always visible

Cost: Free

www.comoroad-go-west.com

Directions: Along Rte. 40 and all over town.

OTHER DINOSAUR DIGGINGS

True dinophiles have plenty to keep them occupied in western Colorado, to say nothing of venturing into nearby Utah. Here are a few of the best:

- **Dinosaur Journey (Museum of Western Colorado).** Be terrified by the region's largest collection of dinosaur robots, touch genuine fossils, and experience a simulated earthquake! (550 Jurassic Ct., Fruita, (888) DIG-DINO, www.dinosaurjourney.org)

- **Dinosaur Valley Museum.** See the ongoing work of resident paleontologists, and view robotic dinosaurs. The museum's collection includes the world's oldest flower fossil. (362 Main St., Grand Junction, (970) 243-3466, www.mwc.mus.co.us)

- **Jurassic Tours, Inc.** Take a five-day, four-night tour of the Dinosaur Diamond region from Fruita southwest to Moab, Utah, northwest to Price, northeast to Vernal, and down through Dinosaur, Rangely, and back to Fruita. (PO Box 626, Fruita, CO 81521, (970) 256-0884, www.jurassictours.com)

- **Rabbit Valley Research Natural Area.** Paleontologists are still removing dinosaurs from this quarry. Join in the fun and dig in the dirt beside paleontologists for $95 per day. (Rabbit Valley, (888) 488-DINO, www.dinodigs.org)

Durango
Butch and Sundance Make the Leap

It's one of those famous scenes that ends up in movie montages during the Academy Awards: Paul Newman and Robert Redford as Butch Cassidy and the Sundance Kid are trapped on a cliff with only one way out: a 30-foot jump to a raging river below. The Sundance Kid admits he can't swim, and Butch reassures him by saying the fall will probably kill him. The pair run off the precipice screaming "Shiiiiiiiiiiiiiiiiiiit!" and escape their pursuers by floating down the rapids.

In reality, the Sundance Kid's nervousness during the shoot might have had little to do with Redford's acting and everything to do with his true feelings at the moment. The actors had to jump off the cliff onto a platform suspended in the chasm, six feet below, and Redford was afraid of heights. The long drop into the Animas River was performed by stuntmen. And the shot of the water where they landed? It was filmed in California.

Baker's Bridge, Rte. 550, Durango, CO 81301

No phone

Hours: Always visible

Cost: Free

Directions: Exactly 11.7 miles north on Rte. 550 from Durango's 32nd St. Junction.

DELTA
Delta calls itself "The City of Murals" because of its public art program.

DINOSAUR
Butch Cassidy's outlaw gang buried $100,000 in a cave on White Mountain near Dinosaur National Monument.

DURANGO
It is against the law in Durango to be seen in public dressed in clothes "unbecoming of one's sex."

Durango & Silverton Narrow Gauge Railroad

The Durango & Silverton has been operating more or less continuously since 1882 when, as the Denver & Rio Grande, it hauled miners and supplies between the two towns. Over the years, miners and ore cars were slowly replaced by tourists and film crews. The 46-mile narrow gauge railroad (tracks 3 feet apart, as opposed to the standard 4 feet, 8.5 inches) has appeared in movies such as *Night Passage* (with Audie Murphy and Jimmy Stewart), *These Thousand Hills*, *A Ticket to Tomahawk* (with Marilyn Monroe), *Denver & Rio Grande*, *How the West Was Won*, and *Around the World in 80 Days* (with everyone). It was also the train robbed in *Butch Cassidy and the Sundance Kid*. If the exploding mail car looked overly violent on screen, it was because the film crew used too much dynamite, much as Butch and Sundance had, nearly killing the stuntmen.

The trip up the Animas River is picturesque, provided you don't hang out the window to see it. If you stick your noggin out on the uphill side of the tracks, you're likely to get it knocked off by a rock outcropping. If you stick it out on the downhill side, you might get a blast of eye-burning cinders from the coal-fired locomotive.

On Memorial Day weekend, the railroad hosts the Iron Horse Bicycle Classic, pitting mountain bikers against the 120-year-old locomotive. During the summer, Silverton stages an Old West–style gunfight on Main Street every evening at 5:30. If you see a gunfight at any other time, dive for cover.

479 Main Ave., Durango, CO 81301

(800) 408-0230 or (970) 247-2733

Hours: May–October, daily 7:30, 8:15, 9:00, and 9:45 A.M.; November–April, daily 10 A.M.

Cost: Adults $41.55 (summer)/$53 (winter); Kids (5–11) $27/$20.80

www.durangotrain.com

Directions: Board on the southern end of Main Ave.

D&SNG Railroad Museum, 479 Main Ave., Durango, CO 81301

(970) 247-2733

Hours: May–October, daily 7 A.M.–8 P.M.; November–April, daily 8 A.M.–5 P.M.

Cost: Adults $5, Kids (5–11) $2.50 (Free with train ride)

Directions: Two blocks east of Rte. 550, two blocks north of Rte. 160.

D&SNG Silverton Railyard Museum, 10th & Animas Sts., Silverton, CO 81433

(970) 387-5416

Hours: May–October, daily 7:30 A.M.–4:30 P.M.

Cost: Adults $5, Kids (5–11) $2.50 (Free with train ride)

Directions: Four blocks east of Rte. 2 on 10th St.

MORE FOR CHOO-CHOO LOVERS

If you still haven't outgrown your train-loving years, here are a few more choo-choos to wet your steam whistle:

- **Cripple Creek & Victor Narrow Gauge Railroad.** Take a four-mile trip past abandoned mines and the ghost town of Anaconda. (520 E. Carr, Cripple Creek, (719) 689-2640, www.cripplecreekrailroad.com)

- **Cumbres & Toltec Scenic Railroad.** A long run, this train services Chama, New Mexico, and Antonito, Colorado, crossing the border 11 times in the 64-mile trip. The opening scenes of *Indiana Jones and the Last Crusade* (with River Phoenix as the young Indy) were filmed on this route. (500 Terrace Ave., Chama, (888) CUMBRES, www.cumbrestoltec.com)

- **Georgetown Loop Railroad.** The railroad's 96-foot-high Devil's Gate trestle circles back over the tracks below on a 4.5-mile journey to the Lebanon Mine and Silver Plume, 1.5 miles away. (1106 Rose St., Georgetown, (800) 691-4FUN, www.georgetownloop.com)

John Wayne Slept Here

"Which way to the ice machine, Pilgrim?" That's what John Wayne might have said as he swaggered through the lobby of the Silver Spur on his occasional visits to Durango. When the Duke was in town, this is where he stayed. What? Did you really think he slept in the wide open spaces, eating campfire beans while being serenaded by coyotes? Do you also believe Arnold Schwarzenegger is a robot from the future? Well . . . you might be right on that one.

Silver Spur, Room 104, 3416 Main Ave., Durango, CO 81301

(800) 847-1715 or (970) 247-1592

E-mail: silverspur@zyx.com

Hours: Always open

Cost: $38–$140/night

www.silver-spur.com

Directions: North of W. 33rd St. on Main Ave. (Rte. 550).

That's gotta hurt!
Photo by author, courtesy of Lyle Nichols

Fruita
Mike the Headless Chicken

Tupelo had Elvis Presley. Seattle had Kurt Cobain. And Fruita had Mike the Headless Chicken.

Mike had a head until September 10, 1945, when farmer Lloyd Olsen chopped it off with the aim of frying Mike up. Olsen wanted to preserve as much of the neck as possible, since that was the part his mother-in-law preferred. It turned out that the neck was all Mike needed, too. After losing his skull, Mike stood up and went around "pecking" for corn as if nothing had happened.

Olsen knew Mike was special, but that a chicken wouldn't get very far without his eyes or beak. So with a change of heart, Olsen started feeding the chicken he'd just tried to murder, one kernel at a time. Mike also "drank" with the aid of an eye dropper.

Several weeks went by, and Mike was doing fine. The local celebrity became a national phenomenon; he appeared in *Life* magazine posed beside his severed head. Olsen hired a manager who took Mike on the road where he appeared with a two-headed cow named Dolly. (Mike had no head, but Dolly had two, so the animal-to-head ratio was correct, said promoters.) The superstar chicken lived for 18 months before its tragic death, on tour, in an Arizona hotel room. The coroner's report said Mike had choked on a corn kernel.

Fruita has never forgotten its native son . . . er . . . rooster. In May 1999, the town threw its first annual Mike the Headless Chicken Festival. Events included a Run Like a Headless Chicken 5K race, Pin the Head on the Chicken, and a Chicken Dance—no brain required. A year later, the Chamber of Commerce hired local welder/sculptor Lyle Nichols to commemorate Mike. Nichols did not charge the city his full fee; he gave them a discount because he didn't have to sculpt a head. (The artist also appears on the cover of this book atop another sculpture, the Chardonnay Chicken, which he made for the Plum Creek Winery in Palisade.)

Aspen Ave. & Mulberry St., Fruita, CO 81521

No phone

E-mail: mike@miketheheadlesschicken.org

Hours: Always visible

Cost: Free

www.miketheheadlesschicken.org

Directions: North two blocks from I-70 (Exit 19), turn right on Aspen Ave., three blocks ahead, on the right.

FRUITA
Fruita has erected a full-size cement dinosaur in a city park at Aspen Ave. and Mesa St.

Big trouble on the *Thelma and Louise* Highway.

Gateway
Thelma and Louise Highway

Only part of this great road movie was shot in the Unaweep Canyon, but you can easily imagine the whole thing being filmed here. You won't see many signs of inhabitants in the 100+ miles from Grand Junction to Nucla, but you will see plenty of cows, rock formations, and sheer drop-offs (often without guardrails).

At the southern end of your drive, stop at the Bedrock General Store (9812 Highway 90, (970) 859-7395). It was from here that Louise phoned the FBI agent played by Harvey Keitel. A short time later, Thelma and Louise were driving off a cliff.

Don't try it—the movie makes it look much more glamorous than it is in reality.

Unaweep Canyon, Rte. 141, Gateway, CO 81522
No phone

Hours: Always visible

Cost: Free

Directions: All along Rte. 141.

Glenwood Springs
Birthplace of the Teddy Bear

In April 1905, President Theodore Roosevelt came to Glenwood Springs to do what he enjoyed most: killin' critters. Specifically, he was looking for a bear—a big bear. During his three-week visit, his base of operations was the Hotel Colorado, known that spring as the Western White House.

Day after day Roosevelt's entourage trudged through the mountains looking for that bear, and day after day that bear eluded him. (He had, however, shot a cub, which his friends claimed was too small for "anything but a doily.") When he returned to the Hotel Colorado, he was noticeably despondent. Worried that the president might leave the state empty-handed, maids at the hotel sewed scraps of cloth together to make a small fake bear. Roosevelt received the stuffed animal on his last day in town, and the pouting chief executive's frown turned upside down.

Roosevelt called it his "doily bear," but a local reporter dubbed the maids' creation a "teddy bear." When the story reached the East Coast, toy manufacturers ran with the idea, and the teddy bear was born. Ironically, Roosevelt's failure to bag a bear in the Rockies resulted in millions of Americans developing childhood attachments to stuffed animals, and lifelong aversions to bear hunts.

Hotel Colorado, 526 Pine St., Glenwood Springs, CO 81601

(800) 544-3998 or (970) 945-6511

E-mail: hotelres@sopris.net

Hours: Always open

Cost: Call for rates

www.hotelcolorado.com

Directions: At the north end of Grand St. (Rte. 82) at 6th St.

GLENWOOD SPRINGS

Each June the town of Glenwood Springs celebrates Strawberry Days at which a Miss Strawberry Days is crowned.

"This is funny!"

Dead Doc Holliday

Doc Holliday, the dentist turned gunslinger, left a trail of dead bodies across the West before he shed this mortal coil. By most accounts, he killed men in Tombstone (Arizona), Dodge City (Kansas), Denver, and Leadville. So you might be tempted to think he perished in a Main Street shoot-out . . . but then you'd be wrong. He died in bed.

Holliday suffered from tuberculosis, and hearing of the supposedly curative powers of the mineral waters at Glenwood Springs, he arrived in May 1887. Doc checked into the Glenwood Hotel (on the northeast corner of Eighth Street & Grand Avenue) and started visiting the pools and caves. They didn't work.

That September Doc slipped into a coma where he languished for almost two months before waking on November 8. Holliday ordered a glass of whiskey, gulped it down, and proclaimed, "This is funny!"

What did he find so hilarious? He'd always told his friends he would never die with his boots off, and there he was, in bed, hovering near death—without his boots! Before he could slip on a pair, he "crossed the Great Divide," Colorado-speak for "kicked the bucket." He was only 36 years old.

Holliday's friends claimed they were worried Doc's body would be stolen by an outlaw gang, so they hid it in the basement of a home that once stood at Eighth Street and Palmer Avenue. (More likely, it was too cold and snowy to cart him to the hilltop cemetery, and they wanted to wait for the spring thaw.) He was later moved to an unmarked grave. A monument has been erected in the Pioneer/Linwood Cemetery, though it's not a headstone as nobody knows where his head is, nor the rest of him, for that matter. The stone is engraved with a six-gun, a poker hand, and the phrase "He died in bed." Rub it in, why don't you?

Fanatic Doc Holliday fans should stop by Doc Holliday's Saloon and Restaurant. It sits on the Glenwood Hotel's old foundation, and is marked with a gigantic neon six-shooter. Also, visit the Frontier Historical Society Museum (1001 Colorado Ave.) to see their collection of Doc-abilia.

Pioneer/Linwood Cemetery, 13th St. & Bennett Ave., Glenwood Springs, CO 81601
No phone
Hours: Daily 8 A.M.–8 P.M.
Cost: Free
www.glenscape.com
Directions: Trail to cemetery starts three blocks east of Grand Ave. at the south end of town.

AND THERE'S MORE . . . MAYBE . . .
Another gunslinger might also be located in an unmarked grave in Glenwood Springs. **Harvey "Kid Curry" Logan** of Butch Cassidy's Hole-in-the-Wall Gang is believed to have committed suicide after being wounded in a shoot-out near Parachute on June 7, 1904. Detractors contend he escaped and fled to South America with Butch Cassidy and the Sundance Kid. Their skepticism is based on his body being identified only by a letter found on the corpse; they think it was planted. Whoever he was, he's buried in the Rosewood Cemetery west of town.

Ted Bundy's Second Colorado Escape

Serial killer Ted Bundy had already escaped once from Colorado law enforcement officials in 1977, but it wouldn't be his last attempt. Following his recapture in Aspen, Bundy was held in the Garfield County Jail where he would soon hatch his next plot. While using his days to tie up the judicial system with requests for changes in venue, he was using his nights to break through a metal panel in the ceiling of his cell. Crawling through the space between the cells' ceilings and the floor above, Bundy was able to make his way to a closet in the unsecured jailer's quarters.

On December 30, after walking out the front door of the facility, Bundy found a sporty MG Midget with the keys in the ignition, drove it to Denver's Stapleton International Airport, and hopped a flight to Chicago. It was lunchtime before the Garfield County jailers realized he was gone.

Garfield County Jail, 701 Colorado Ave., Glenwood Springs, CO 81601

(970) 945-0453

Hours: Always visible

Cost: Free

Directions: One block west of Grand Ave., just south of the river.

GRAND JUNCTION

Grand Junction's suicide prevention hot line was once a 900 number costing 25¢ for the first minute and $2.50 for every minute thereafter.

Author/screenwriter **Dalton Trumbo** grew up in Grand Junction, and memorialized his hometown in many novels as Shale City. He was later a victim of the House Un-American Activities Committee.

Cowboy **Jimmy Dale Stubble** was buried in a Grand Junction cemetery standing up. Stubble had been paralyzed years earlier in a barroom fight.

Vapor Caves

If you've ever wanted Mother Earth to wrap her arms around you, to be enveloped in the bowels of the Great Spirit, come to the Yampah Spa and Vapor Caves, the only natural vapor caves in North America. Discovered by the Utes, miners and trappers began to make use of the steamy caves along the Grand River (later renamed the Colorado River) to ease their aching bones. And why not? *Yampah* means "big medicine."

The current caves are actually the third in a succession of caves that have been closed or destroyed by railroad and highway construction. To get to the caves, you must enter through a New Agey spa that offers massage, herbal wraps, and other soothing remedies, all the while serenaded by the sound of wind chimes, breaking waves, and prancing unicorns.

The caves themselves are a little more rustic. As you descend the steps your nose will tell you that you are indeed entering the bowels of the Earth, not unlike a human suppository. Recline on the marble benches, installed in 1883, and relax to the drip, drip, drip of the hot mineral waters seeping out of the walls. Sure, it smells bad, but it feels sooooo good!

Yampah Spa and Vapor Caves, 709 E. Sixth Ave., Glenwood Springs, CO 81601

(970) 945-0667

E-mail: yampahspa@sopris.net

Hours: Daily 9 A.M.–9 P.M.

Cost: $7

www.yampahhotsprings.com/caves.html

Directions: East of the Hot Springs Pool, just north of I-70.

World's Largest Outdoor Hot Springs

It's hard to convince those who have never taken a dip in the Glenwood Hot Springs to jump into the stinky water—almost as difficult as it is to get them to come out after they've given it a try—and for good reason. Because it is the World's Largest Outdoor Hot Springs Pool, it's easy to find a secluded place to relax without bumping into naked hippies and children playing Marco Polo. Try doing that at a rustic mountain hot spring or your neighborhood pool.

The Glenwood Springs Hot Pool is two blocks long, 100 feet across at its widest point, and holds a million gallons of water. It is fed by an

adjacent 122-degree mineral spring at the rate of 3.5 million gallons a day. Carefully mixed, the large pool maintains a constant temperature of 90 degrees, while the smaller hot pool, known to some (affectionately) as the Walrus Pond, is 104 degrees.

The pool opened in 1888; the original spring and river were diverted using inmate labor from this once rough-and-tumble mining town. The structure on the south side of the pool was completed in 1890, and was the original bathhouse. It included a gambling casino for the town's towel-draped upper crust. An Inhalatorium was also built so folks could breathe concentrated clouds of the supposedly curative sulfur steam. It has since been torn down.

The best time to visit the hot springs is in the dead of winter. The crowds have died down, the billows of steam make an eerie wonderland, and you just might bump into the pool's resident ghost, Agnes, in the locker room. She is said to walk the halls, slam doors, and flush toilets whenever the notion strikes her. If you think you're being watched, you're probably right.

Hot Springs Lodge and Pool, 401 N. River Rd., PO Box 308, Glenwood Springs, CO 81601
(800) 537-SWIM or (970) 945-6571
Hours: Daily; Winters 9 A.M.–10 P.M.; Summers 7:30 A.M.–10 P.M.
Cost: Adults $9.50, Kids (3–12) $6.25
www.hotspringspool.com
Directions: East of Grand Ave., just north of I-70.

Hotchkiss
Death Site of David Letterman's "Wife"

When 46-year-old Margaret Mary Ray knelt on the railroad tracks in Hotchkiss on October 5, 1998, it was the final act in a sad and bizarre life.

Ray first entered David Letterman's life in 1988 when she was seen tooling down the Connecticut tollway in Letterman's Porsche, introducing herself to booth tellers as Mrs. David Letterman and pointing to the young boy beside her saying, "That's David Junior!" Well, it wasn't. And neither was the car hers. She'd stolen it from Letterman's New Canaan home.

Though she never made any attempt to *harm* Letterman, she did want to be *near* him. In 1992 Ray broke into his estate while he was home, and on another occasion left a gift of cookies and whiskey in his garage.

Her infatuation abated only when she developed a new crush on former astronaut Story Musgrave. Ray was convinced he'd impregnated her telepathically. She was arrested in September 1997 for trespassing at Musgrave's home in Kissimmee, Florida.

Ray served a total of 31 months behind bars for numerous violations related to Letterman and Musgrave. It all ended when the coal train rumbled through Hotchkiss and over the troubled 46-year-old stalker. Friends scattered her ashes at nearby Needle Rock.

Route 92, Hotchkiss, CO 81419

No phone

Hours: Always visible

Cost: Free

Directions: North of Rte. 92, along the railroad tracks.

GRAND JUNCTION

The World's Tallest Unicycle is currently in the possession of the Museum of Western Colorado (Ute & Fifth Sts., (970) 242-0971, www.wcmuseum.org), but against all good judgment, *they do not have it on display!*

MANCOS

Jaye P. Morgan of *The Gong Show* grew up in Mancos.

MARBLE

The marble for the Lincoln Memorial and the Tomb of the Unknowns (in Arlington National Cemetery) was quarried along Yule Creek, four miles from Marble.

MAYBELL

Colorado's lowest recorded temperature was -61°F on February 1, 1985, in Maybell.

Who are you calling a dummy?

Loma
Hangin' Time

You're barreling north on Route 139, building up a head of steam as you hit the first uphill grade on Douglas Pass, and you look over to the east to see a body hanging from a long-dead cottonwood tree. Is vigilante justice alive in Colorado? you wonder. Is this the end for some cattle-rustlin' varmint? Or a suicide, perhaps?

A firm believer in due process, you hit the brakes, turn around, and head back to a gravel pull-off on the right shoulder. And then you see a small hand-painted sign hanging on a metal gate at the turn-off: "It's a dummy, dummy." Ha-ha-ha-ha-ha. You hop back in your car and head north, your engine groaning up the hill, struggling to recover from the dead stop.

Posses may be a thing of the past, but if they were organizing one to hunt down that smart-ass SOB who put up that sign, chances are you'd gladly saddle up.

Douglas Pass, Rte. 139, Loma, CO 81524

No phone

Hours: Always visible

Cost: Free

Directions: North of town on Rte. 139, just past mile marker 20, look to the east.

MONTROSE
Drivers in Montrose cannot hang their bare feet out their car windows.

OURAY
If you have smallpox or another contagious disease, your stagecoach driver must dump you five miles outside Ouray.

By law, you have six hours to remove a freshly dead animal from Ouray's city limits.

Ouray calls itself "The Switzerland of America."

Truck-drivin' singer **C. W. McCall** was once mayor of Ouray. His real name is Bill Fries.

Wait until you see the Indians . . .

Mancos
Rain of Arrows

Cruising along Route 160 west of Mancos, you'll suddenly be overcome with a shrinking feeling. Jabbed into the ground beside a roadside trinket store is a quiverful of 30-foot arrows. They stand beside several shorter wooden tipis, so the native inhabitants couldn't have been the ones that fired them. Then who made these weapons out of telephone poles and attacked this peace-loving trading post? We may never know.

Mud Creek Hogan, 38651 Rte. 160, Mancos, CO 81328

(970) 533-7117

Hours: Always visible

Cost: Free

Directions: West of town on Rte. 160.

Meeker
The End of the Junior Wild Bunch

Three young former members of Butch Cassidy's Wild Bunch—Jim Shirley, George Bain (also known as George Low, George Law, or George Harvies), and "The Kid" Pearce (also known as Billy Smith), tried to rob the Bank of Meeker (Main and 6th Streets) in broad daylight on October 13, 1896. But, with inexplicable amateurish enthusiasm, they fired two warning shots over the head of a teller to prove they meant business.

These shots were also a signal to the rest of the town to gather their firearms and meet over at the bank. When the trio emerged, they were promptly gunned down by the local population. Their good-fer-nothin' bodies were laid out on public display, then buried in a local cemetery, where you can see their headstones today.

Highland Cemetery, County Road 62, Meeker, CO 81641
No phone
Hours: Always visible
Cost: Free
Directions: South of town 0.5 miles on 10th St. (County Rd. 62), turn south just after
the bridge.

He Had It Coming . . .

Nathan Meeker pushed his luck. As the Indian Agent in northwest Colorado, he had tried to force White River Utes to become farmers, and forbade them from hunting, fishing, and horseback racing. He insisted the Utes address him as Father Meeker. He even threatened to cut off food rations if they didn't start plowing and irrigating. In an effort to push them into an agricultural lifestyle, he had their primary horse pasture and race course plowed up and laid out with irrigation ditches. He then sent for troops from Fort Fred Steele in Wyoming to help enforce his edicts.

That was the last straw. On September 29, 1879, the Utes fought back. Meeker and nine of his employees were killed in an attack led by Chief Douglass. It became known as the Meeker Massacre. Nathan Meeker met a uniquely grisly end; he was held down and a wooden stake was driven through his mouth. Why? "To silence his infernal lying," Ute sub-Chief Colorow observed matter-of-factly.

Meeker's wife and daughter were taken hostage along with three others. The troops summoned from Wyoming were attacked near Milk Creek (20 miles northeast of town), and in the ensuing battles 14 troopers died, including commander Thomas Thornburgh. The hostages were eventually released, and the White River Utes were forcibly moved to a reservation in Utah.

The Army set up camp on White River, which eventually became the town of Meeker. A museum is now housed in the former officers' quarters, and includes Colorow's flintlock rifle and peace pipe.

Meeker Massacre Site, Rte. 64, Meeker, CO 81641

No phone

Hours: Always visible

Cost: Free

www.meekerchamber.com/historical.htm

Directions: Three miles west of town on Rte. 64.

White River Museum, 565 Park St., PO Box 413, Meeker, CO 81641

(970) 878-9982

Hours: April–October, Monday–Friday 9 A.M.–5 P.M.; November–March, Monday–Friday 11 A.M.–3 P.M.

Cost: Free

Directions: Between 4th and 5th Sts., two blocks north of Rte. 13.

New Castle
Burning Mountain

The Vulcan Mine, just across the Colorado River from New Castle, has had a long, disaster-filled safety record. An explosion there on February 18, 1896, killed 49 miners. Because there was a considerable amount of coal still to be extracted, the Vulcan was quickly reopened. The tragedy repeated itself in 1913 when another blast killed 37.

Yet another accident occurred on November 4, 1918. This time however, the fire forced the mine to close, and it will likely never reopen—because it's still burning! That's right, more than 80 years after it began, coal veins inside the mountain still smolder. And if you need any evidence, visit New Castle during the winter. Snow does not collect on various patches atop Burning Mountain where the ground is warmed by fires below.

I-70, New Castle, CO 81647

No phone

Hours: Always visible; winters best

Cost: Free

Directions: Look south across the river and interstate from New Castle.

Rangely
Carrot Men!

It sounds frightening, but long ago creatures shaped like gigantic carrots roamed this corner of Colorado. Why else would there be so many carrot-shaped petroglyphs on the walls of Moon Canyon? Anthropologists believe these rock art images date back to the Fremont Culture, which lived in the region between A.D. 650 and 1150. They're located on the underside of a rock overhang in a dry gully not far from the picnic area, and though they are in as remote a location as you're likely to find, they're still on the National Register of Historic Places.

So who were these Carrot Men? Vegetarian gods? Mutant roots? Or was the Fremont Culture foreshadowing Pee Wee's Playhouse fridge?

Carrot Men Site, Moon Canyon, 23 Rd., Rangely, CO 81648

Contact: Rangely Outdoor Museum, PO Box 131, Rangely, CO 81648

(970) 675-2612

Hours: Always visible

Cost: Free

Directions: South of town on 23 Road at milepost 11.6.

RIDGWAY

The western town scenes in *True Grit* were filmed on Ridgway's main street.

RIFLE

Rifle brags that it is "Oil Shale Capital of the World."

SILVERTON

The song "There'll Be a Hot Time on the Old Town Tonight" was written in Silverton, for Silverton.

The U.S. Atmospheric Survey claims that the nation's cleanest air is on Molas Pass south of Silverton.

TELLURIDE

Twenty-three miners and their rescuers were killed in a pair of avalanches in the winter of 1907 near Telluride. The avalanches occurred at the Liberty Bell area east of town.

George Leroy Parker, also known as **Butch Cassidy**, and a gang of three others robbed the San Miguel Valley Bank (it burned down in 1892) in Telluride on June 24, 1884. They got $10,500; $2,200 of it went to town marshal Jim Clark who was conveniently out of town at the time. It was Butch Cassidy's first job. Hollywood returned in 1969 to film scenes of *Butch Cassidy and the Sundance Kid* at the New Sheridan Hotel (231 Colorado Ave.).

Skiing first came to Telluride when miners from the Tomboy Mine raced 3,000 feet down the mountain to get the first pick of the brothel women on payday.

Each July, Telluride hosts the Nothing Festival where participants do just that: nothing. Visit www.telluridenothingfestival.com to find out what won't be happening.

"You ride to hell." That's what miners near Telluride would say of the trip to town because it was so wild.

William Jennings Bryan delivered his "Cross of Gold" speech on July 4, 1896, in front of Telluride's New Sheridan Hotel (231 Colorado Ave., (970) 728-4351).

Rifle
Big Busy Beaver

Long before Hoover Dam was even conceived, another gigantic construction project was undertaken along Colorado's East Rifle Creek . . . by a beaver! This creature began building its dam thousands of years ago and soon reached 10, then 20, then 30 feet high. It didn't stop, and piled logs and branches higher and higher like the Tower of Babel until it was 10 stories tall!

Minerals in the water flowing over the dam calcified the wood, eventually forming the limestone outcropping that today is called Rifle Falls. Though today we do not know the name of that enterprising rodent, we can still marvel at its superbeaver achievement.

Rifle Falls State Park, Rte. 325, Rifle, CO 81650

(970) 625-1607

Hours: Daylight hours

Cost: Free

parks.state.co.us/rifle_falls

Directions: Three miles northeast of Rifle Gap Reservoir along Rte. 325.

Torn Valley Curtain

It didn't last long, but *Valley Curtain* thrust Czech-born artist Christo into the artistic spotlight quicker than any modern artist ever before. It happened on August 10, 1972. A 142,000-square-foot, orange nylon curtain was dropped into place from cables stretched across Rifle Gap, a 1,250-foot break in the Grand Hogback seven miles north of Rifle.

It was the culmination of two years of planning and $700,000, and the workers who installed it that morning celebrated their success by throwing the overjoyed artist into Rifle Creek. Though it had been designed to stay in place for a month, 60-MPH winds the next day ripped the nine-ton curtain to shreds, and the curtain fell on *Valley Curtain*.

Christo went on to wrap Berlin's Reichstag in 1995, encircle 11 islands in Miami's Biscayne Bay with pink plastic, run a 24.5-mile-long nylon "fence" into the Pacific Ocean, and accidentally crush a California tourist when one of his two-story yellow umbrellas blew over in the wind, landing on the unfortunate art lover.

Rifle Gap State Park, Rte. 325, Rifle, CO 81650

(970) 625-1607

Hours: Always visible

Cost: Free

www.christojeanneclaude.net/christo/xtojc/vc.html

Directions: North from town three miles on Rte. 13, turn right on Rte. 325, and drive three miles to the gap in the Grand Hogback.

THE SECOND COMING OF CHRISTO

He shall return . . . unless some folks in Salida have something to say about it! If all goes as planned, Christo will suspend 6.7 miles of semi-transparent woven fabric panels over the Arkansas River for two weeks in the summer of 2004. Called *Over the River*, the work will trace the riverbed. It will hang 10 to 23 feet above the water, and make way for trees, bridges, and rock outcroppings. Local residents, who depend on the Arkansas for tourism and recreation, are not enthusiastic about the project, and have moved to block its installation. Stay tuned for details: www.christojeanneclaude.net/christo/otr/otr.html

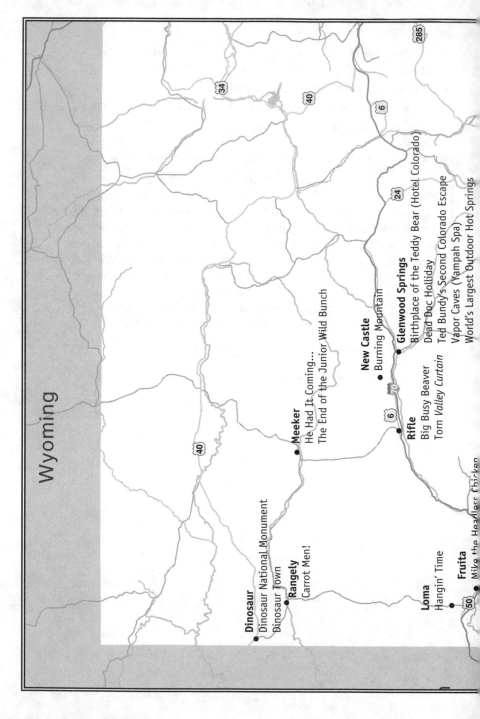

Wyoming

Dinosaur
Dinosaur National Monument
Dinosaur Town

Rangely
Carrot Men!

Meeker
He Had It Coming...
The End of the Junior Wild Bunch

New Castle
Burning Mountain

Glenwood Springs
Birthplace of the Teddy Bear (Hotel Colorado)
Dead Doc Holliday
Ted Bundy's Second Colorado Escape
Vapor Caves (Yampah Spa)
World's Largest Outdoor Hot Springs

Rifle
Big Busy Beaver
Torn *Valley Curtain*

Loma
Hangin' Time

Fruita
Mike the Headless Chicken

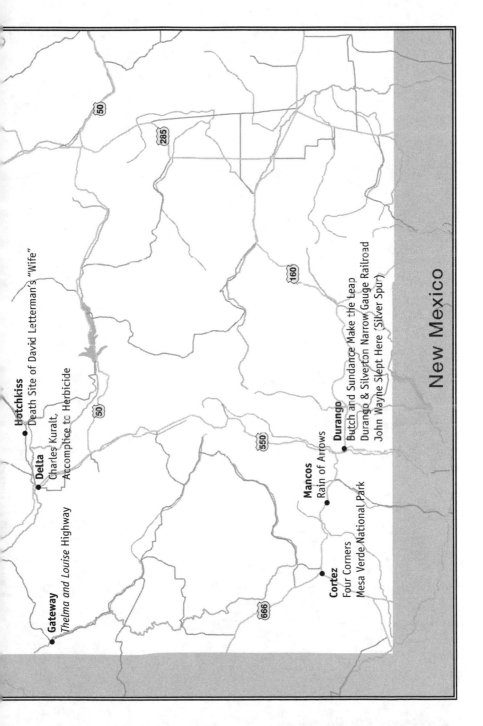

Hotchkiss
Death Site of David Letterman's "Wife"

Delta
Charles Kuralt, Accomplice to Herbicide

Gateway
Thelma and Louise Highway

Mancos
Rain of Arrows

Durango
Butch and Sundance Make the Leap
Durango & Silverton Narrow Gauge Railroad
John Wayne Slept Here ('Silver Spur')

Cortez
Four Corners
Mesa Verde National Park

New Mexico

6

THE OUTHOUSE TOUR

*I*t is hard to underestimate the importance of outhouses to the growth of the state of Colorado. There just weren't enough trees on the eastern plains and the western slope to hide behind. And although there were plenty of trees in the mountains, who wanted to litter the beautiful scenery with human doo-doo? North, south, east, or west—Colorado needed outhouses. Most were garden-variety privies, but others were odd and fantastic. Several of them can still be seen today. They're the focus of this brief theme tour.

Oh, it may sound strange to go out of your way to look at a toilet built in the 1800s, but the outhouse still has an emotional hold on some parts of the state. The toughest ski run at Arapaho Basin is called Outhouse. The town of Black Forest, just northeast of Colorado Springs, holds an annual Outhouse Race where crappers are placed on wheels and pushed through town. Believe me, this is one race where *nobody* wants to see a wreck. Similar logic is behind a law that's still on the books in Ouray: residents can only empty their privies between midnight and 5 A.M.

So come along, and bring your camera. Nobody back at the office will believe you spent your vacation looking down the hole of an outhouse. You'll want documentation.

Look out below!

Crested Butte
Double-Decker Outhouse

Tacked on to the backside of a Crested Butte art gallery is a pink-trimmed, two-seater outhouse. This would not necessarily be remarkable were it not that seats are placed one over the other. Well, not *exactly*, but fairly close. The ground-level unit was accessed through an outer door (popular in summer), while the second-floor unit was attached to the building through an upper walkway (popular in winter).

This architectural oddity is made possible, and functional, by offsetting the first-floor seat from the second-floor hole. Both back up to a common wall that leads to a single pit below. The gallery no longer uses either of the crappers, but maintains the outer structure for history's sake. We should all be grateful for their efforts.

Diamond/Tanita Gallery, 311 Elk Ave., Crested Butte, CO 81224

(970) 349-0940

Hours: Always visible

Cost: Free

Directions: In the alley to the north, behind the gallery.

Alma
Hidgepath's Bones

When he was alive, J. Dawson Hidgepath fancied himself a Casanova. Nobody else shared his opinion. The miner employed a strategy of calling on any and every member of the female persuasion to ask for her hand in marriage, be she single, spoken for, hitched, widowed, underage, or one foot in the grave. The constant rejections didn't seem to bother him, he just moved on to the next available woman—and by "available" he meant breathing and within eyesight.

Hidgepath's quest seemingly came to an abrupt end when he fell off nearby Mount Bross in 1865. Seemingly. Not long after his mangled corpse was found at the bottom of a rockslide and buried in Buckskin Joe Cemetery, his bones showed up on the bed of a prostitute in nearby Alma. Locals identified the skeleton by the hat that sat atop the skull; it was Hidgepath's!

The miner was no sooner reburied than he reappeared in the bed of a new woman—but this one was happily married. Again, his remains were accompanied by the telltale hat. Back to the cemetery went the bones, yet the graveyard could not contain the determined dead suitor. Every few months for several years he'd reappear, each time to court a different unlucky female.

Townsfolk finally came up with a drastic, devious, and dirty plan to put an end to Hidgepath's shenanigans, and it involved outhouses. The next time the bones appeared, they were divided among volunteers who took them home and tossed them into their respective outhouses. That seemed to do the trick.

Still, there's no guarantee. Hidgepath's headstone in the abandoned Buckskin Joe Cemetery marks an empty grave. If you're female and traveling through the area, don't be so quick to blame the motel if your bed contains some smelly human bones. You might be being courted.

Buckskin Joe Cemetery, Buckskin Gulch Rd. (Fire Rd. 416), Alma, CO 80440

No phone

Hours: Always visible

Cost: Free

Directions: Two miles west of Alma near the old ghost town of Buckskin Joe (also known as Laurette).

Georgetown
Now That's a Throne!

If you have no choice but to build an outhouse, if indoor plumbing is out of the question no matter how much money you have, you might as well go all out. If crapper it is, make it king of all crappers.

Such was the philosophy of William Arthur Hamill, Georgetown silver baron. He bought a home on the south side of town from his brother-in-law, Joseph Watson, in 1874, and five years later began rehabbing the place with an enthusiasm that would put most of today's urban pioneers to shame. A carriage house, a stable, an office, and quarters for his servants were added . . . *and* a much improved outhouse.

Greek Revival it is—no half-moon cut-out for the Hamill family! The outhouse can seat six at a time on its solid oak seats: four family members and two servants. Following Victorian protocol, the servants' holes are accessed through a different door than the family's. The structure has a porch, a cornice, and a cupola.

Hamill's throne *was* his castle!

Hamill House Museum, 305 Argentine St., Georgetown, CO 80444

(303) 569-2840

E-mail: preservation@historicgeorgetown.org

Hours: June–September, daily 10 A.M.–4 P.M.
Cost: Adults $5, Seniors $4, Kids (under 7) Free
www.historicgeorgetown.org
Directions: At the south end of town at 3rd St.

EPiLOGUe

*I*t always pains me to bring the bad news, which is why I always wait until the end of the book: roadside oddities are a dying breed. The wonderfully weird folk in this guide are fighting an uphill battle against the elements, poachers of nonconformity, real estate developers, and folks who have crowned themselves high priests and priestesses of good taste.

The Centennial State has a sad oddball history. Take the case of Pueblo's Colorado Mineral Palace, ruled over by Old King Coal, a statue carved from anthracite, and his wife, the Silver (Plated) Queen. This 1890 structure was made of wood and simulated stone, and was intended as a monument to the state's mining industry. Had the builders used real stone, the WPA might not have had to tear down the crumbling palace in 1936.

Poor planning for the harsh elements is one thing, but it's even more difficult to forecast the changing American taste. Such was the fate of the once-popular mummified remains of Tom O'Neal. Dr. Isaac Davis preserved the dead, drunken gambler during one of the gold rushes, and parked the pickled carcass outside his Manitou Springs pharmacy. Can you see anything like that these days? Noooo, because somebody might complain.

It's the same kind of do-gooder mentality that doomed the Tropics burlesque house in Denver (at Sheridan Blvd. & Morrison Rd.). Residents bellyached about the smarmy crowd attracted by the strippers, yet said nothing about the club's wonder-filled interior; the Tropics had indoor lightning, thunder, and rain that sprinkled from pipes along the ceiling. Ditto for Debbie Duz Donuts, a topless donut shop in Fort Collins. After opening with much national attention in 1989—OK, it was mostly from *Geraldo*—the one-of-a-kind pastry shop drew local protests and closed within a year.

Apathy and economics have killed even more sites. The sun has set on Cañon City's Sunset Drive-In Theater with its unique playground located just below the expansive CinemaScope screen. No longer can you watch both the movie and the kids at the same time. The Convair Restaurant at the Tri-County Airport in Erie has crashed as well. Housed in the fuselage of a grounded Convair 900, the 140-foot plane didn't draw the customers it needed, so today it's in a hangar. And what happened to the eight robotic cowboys at the Brass Ass Saloon in Cripple Creek? Make way for more slot machines . . . and a far less interesting tourist destination.

Still more difficult to understand are the attractions that have been killed before they've gotten off the drawing board. In 1964 a plan was drafted to build a World Science Tower just north of Larkspur. The tower was to be the tallest building in the world, and have an amusement park at its base. Don't bother looking—it was killed before anyone broke ground. And what does Larkspur have today? Not much.

If the message isn't clear, I'll dispense with the subtleties: see roadside oddities while you can—you may never get a second chance. We might hope to live in a world where 42-foot hot dogs and headless chicken festivals and alligator colonies last forever, but that's a fantasy. Get up, smell the coffee, get into your car, and drive, drive, drive!

ACKNOWLEDGMENTS

On August 16, 1964, my parents moved our family from California to Colorado. Our first night in the Centennial State was spent in a tourist cabin in the unincorporated village of No Name, just east of Glenwood Springs. Though I do not remember it (I was one and a half years old at the time), my parents say my brothers and I awoke the next morning, heard the sound of a creek behind the cabin, and demanded to go outside and take a look. Not even a day into the state, I had already begun my research.

First day on the job. Author (left) and brothers Jim (center) and Joe.

Colorado was a great place to grow up. One of my earliest childhood memories was seeing a re-enactment of the Meeker Massacre at a Granby rodeo. Burning wagons, Indians on horseback . . . it was fantastic! Summers were filled with visits to the public pool at the defunct Wolhurst

Country Club, a pool I loved because it was filled with frogs from the adjacent Hi-Line Canal. Our family camped often at the Great Sand Dunes, choked down dust at the Pikes Peak Hill Climb, and soaked in the Glenwood Springs pool in the dead of winter. My brothers and I believed (and we were right!) that fine dining consisted of the Denver Drumstick, a restaurant on Santa Fe Drive with a model train running on a track near the ceiling; Food King, a Littleton eatery where you ordered from a phone at your table; the Yum-Yum Tree food bazaar, a stand-alone food court before there were food courts; and Casa Bonita, the ultimate birthday party destination. Sadly, only the latter establishment survives today.

My parents knew the value of travel, why it was important to explore all the state and the country had to offer. Every year was filled with new adventures in our big orange Dodge, and I remember every trip. I owe my parents so much. In particular I owe them for this book. They gave me what my grandmother called "itchy feet." Thank you both, for everything.

This book would not have been possible without the assistance, patience, and good humor of many individuals. My thanks go out to the following people for allowing me to interview them about their roadside attractions: Laura Lee Amman (Solid Muldoon/Beulah Historical Society), Jon Barnes (The Ultimate Taxi), Jerry Chubbock (Wonder View Tower), Peggy Ford (Rattlesnake Kate/Greeley Museums), Tom Haggard (North Pole/Santa's Workshop), Bob "Doc" Honeywell (John S. Stewart VFW Post #1), Rebecca Jackson (Turin Shroud Center of Colorado), Winston Jones (International Bell Museum), Pat Kant (Museum of Colorado Prisons), Marie Kaufman (Traildust Steak House), Hedwig Kempf (Kempf's Kreations), Esther Mellott (National Mining Hall of Fame and Museum), Sid and Renae Levin (The Buckhorn Exchange), Daphne Rice-Allen (Black American West Museum & Heritage Center), Judy Messoline (UFO Watchtower), Bill Swets (Swetsville Zoo), and Lynne Young (Colorado Alligator Farm).

For research assistance, I am indebted to the librarians in the Colorado communities of Alamosa, Denver, Eads, Fort Collins, Greeley, Lafayette, Littleton, Longmont, Meeker, and Pueblo. Thanks also to the Visitors Bureaus and/or Chambers of Commerce in Cañon City, Creede, Durango, Estes Park, Fairplay, Fruita, Georgetown, Glenwood Springs, Idaho Springs, Lake City, Lamar, Leadville, Manitou Springs, San Luis, and Sterling. Several of this book's historic photographs were made possible with the pleasant and professional assistance of the Colorado Historical Society/Stephen H. Hart Library and the Denver Public Library Photography Collection. To my research assistants, Mom and Dad, thanks for the trips to NORAD, the Denver Public Library, and Mattie's House of Mirrors.

Friends, family members, and strangers willingly volunteered (sometimes after excessive badgering on my part) to act as models for the photographs in this book: Maureen Bachmann, Jon Barnes, Jim Frost, Jim Pohlen, Matthew Pohlen, Eric Pohlen, Daniel Pohlen, and Joe Pohlen. Artist Lyle Nichols posed atop the chicken he created, which is on the book's cover; the photo was taken by David "D. B." Cooper. Thanks everyone.

Many thanks to the staff at Chicago Review Press for encouraging and developing the Oddball travel series. To the gang at WBEZ, Chicago Public Radio, for supporting Cool Spots, my deepest appreciation.

To a Colorado friend who I've known since third grade, Gordon Wells, thank you for keeping me on my intellectual toes. To my teachers in the Douglas County public schools, especially Yvonne Tricarico, Olive Larson, Rosemary Metzler, Steven Williams, Wally Larsen, Marty Bowen, Jodene Bartolo (Kissler), Doug Kissler, Kathleen Gilbert, and Stephen Wright, you all deserved so much more than the county's stingy voters ever gave you, as they defeated bond measures year, after year, after year. I couldn't have asked for a better education. And to Robert Johnson at the University of Colorado at Denver, thank you for encouraging my writing.

Finally, to Jim Frost, who has been with me from that first trip to Racine, Wisconsin, my deepest gratitude.

ReCOMMeNDeD SouRces

If you'd like to learn more about the places and individuals in this book, the following are excellent sources.

Introduction

General Colorado Guides
Colorado by Carl Abbott, Stephen Leonard, and David McComb (Boulder, CO: Colorado Associated University Press, 1982)

Colorado Off the Beaten Path by Curtis Casewit (Old Saybrook, CT: Globe Pequot Press, 1999)

It Happened in Colorado by James A. Crutchfield (Helena, MT: Falcon Publishing, Inc., 1993)

Colorado Museums and Historic Sites by Victor Danilov (Boulder, CO: University Press of Colorado, 2000)

Tours for Free in Colorado by Jodi Jill (Boulder, CO: BentLight Media, 2001)

Colorado: A History in Photographs by Dan Klinglesmith and Patrick Soran (Denver, CO: Altitude Publishing, Ltd., 1998)

Roadside History of Colorado by James McTighe (Boulder, CO: Johnson Books, 1989)

Quick Escapes from Denver by Sherry Spitsnaugle (Old Saybrook, CT: Globe Pequot Press, 2000)

Colorado Historical Tour Guide by D. Ray Wilson (Carpentersville, IL: Crossroads Communications, 1990)

Colorado Trivia
Colorado's Gold Mines and Buried Treasure by Caroline Bancroft (Boulder, CO: Bancroft Books, 1961)

1001 Colorado Place Names by Maxine Benson (Lawrence, KS: University of Kansas Press, 1994)

Colorado's Colorful Characters by Gladys R. Bueler (Boulder, CO: Pruett Publishing, 1981)

I Never Knew That About Colorado by Abbott Fay (Ouray, CO: Western Reflections, 1997)

More That I Never Knew About Colorado by Abbott Fay (Ouray, CO: Western Reflections, 2000)

Bizarre Colorado by Kenneth Jensen (Loveland, CO: J. V. Publications, 1994)

Eccentric Colorado by Kenneth Jensen (Loveland, CO: J. V. Publications, 1985)

Unique Colorado by Sarah Lovett (Santa Fe, NM: John Muir Publications, 1993)

Colorado Trivia by B. J. Murphey-Lenahan (Nashville, TN: Rutledge Hill, 1991)

The Colorado Almanac by Thomas J. Noel (Portland, OR: Westwinds Press, 2001)

From the Grave by Linda Wommack (Caldwell, ID: Caxton Press, 1998)

Colorado Ghosts

Mysteries & Miracles of Colorado by Jack Kutz (Corrales, NM: Rhombus Publishing, 1993)

Twilight Dwellers of Colorado by MaryJoy Martin (Boulder, CO: Pruett Publishing, 1985)

1. Denver Area

Denver (General)

Denver in Slices by Louisa Ward Arps (Athens, OH: Swallow Press, 1959)

Places Around the Bases by Diane Bakke and Jackie Davis (Englewood, CO: Westcliffe Publishers, 1995)

Denver in Our Time by Phil Goodstein (Denver, CO: New Social Publications, 1999)

The Seamy Side of Denver by Phil Goodstein (Denver, CO: New Social Publications, 1993)

African Americans in the West

The Black West by William Loren Katz (New York: Touchstone, 1996)

Buffalo Bill
Buffalo Bill: Myth and Reality by Eric Sorg (Santa Fe, NM: Ancient City Press, 1998)

DIA
DIA and Other Scams by Phil Goodstein (Denver, CO: New Social Publications, 2000)

The Murder of Alan Berg
Talked to Death by Stephen Singular (New York: Beech Tree Books, 1987)

Neil Bush and Silverado
"Banking on Savings and Loans," in *DIA and Other Scams* by Phil Goodstein (Denver, CO: New Social Publications, 2000)

Riverside Cemetery
Walk Through Historical Riverside Cemetery by the Fairmount Heritage Foundation (Denver, CO: Self-Published, 2001)

Roseanne
My Life as a Woman by Roseanne Barr (New York: Harper and Row, 1989)
My Lives by Roseanne (New York: Ballantine Books, 1994)

Unsinkable Molly Brown
The Unsinkable Mrs. Brown by Caroline Bancroft (Boulder, CO: Johnson Books, 1961)

Ad Coors's Kidnapping
Citizen Coors by Dan Baum (New York: Perennial, 2000)

2. Eastern Colorado and the Front Range

The Solid Muldoon
From Mace's Hole, the Way It Was, to Beulah, the Way It Is by the Beulah Historical Society (Beulah, CO: Self-Published, 2000)

Kit Carson County Carousel

Kit Carson County Carousel: PTC #6 Story by Anonymous (Burlington, CO: Kit Carson County Carousel, Date Unknown)

Sand Creek Massacre

Attack on Black Kettle's Village and the Prelude to Sand Creek by Ruth Dunn (Julesburg, CO: Self-Published, 1973)

The Sand Creek Massacre by Stan Hoig (Norman, OK: University of Oklahoma Press, 1961)

Song of Sorrow by Patrick M. Mendoza (Denver, CO: Willow Wind Publishing Company, 1993)

Blood at Sand Creek by Bob Scott (Caldwell, ID: Caxton Printers, Ltd., 1994)

Swetsville Zoo

The Swetsville Zoo by Kerry Davis (Self-Published, Date Unknown)

Glenn Miller's Early Days

A Boy . . . a Golden Trombone . . . and a Dream by Tom Yates (Fort Morgan, CO: Ft. Morgan Museum, 1996)

Rattlesnake Kate

"The Story of Rattlesnake Kate" by Peggy Ford (Mt. Morris, IL: *Piecework*, March/April 2000)

The Towner Bus Tragedy

Children of the Storm by Ariana Harner and Clark Secrest (Golden, CO: Fulcrum Publishing, 2001)

Jules Beni and Julesburg

The Burning of Julesburg by Ruth Dunn (Julesburg, CO: Self-Published, 1973)

Indian Vengeance at Julesburg by Ruth Dunn (Julesburg, CO: Self-Published, 1972)

The Ludlow Massacre
Mother Jones: The Most Dangerous Woman in America by Linda Atkinson
(New York: Crown, 1978)

Bridey Murphy
The Search for Bridey Murphy by Morey Berstein (New York: Doubleday,
1956)

Shamballa Ashrama and the Brotherhood of the White Temple
Kooks by Donna Kossy (Portland, OR: Feral House, 1994)

3. Colorado Springs Area

Pikes Peak
America's Mountain by Richard M. Pearl (Colorado Springs, CO: Little
London Press, 1964)
*America the Beautiful: The Stirring True Story Behind Our Nation's
Favorite Song* by Lynn Sherr (New York: Public Affairs, 2001)

Garden of the Gods
Garden of Gods by Paul W. Nesbit (Boulder, CO: Self-Published, 1996)

Nikola Tesla
Tesla: Man Out of Time by Margaret Cheney (New York: Laurel, 1981)
My Inventions by Nikola Tesla (New York: Barnes & Noble Books, 1992)

Cave of the Winds
Without Rival by Richard Rhinehart (Virginia Beach, VA: Donning Company, 2000)

The Texas 7
The Texas 7 by Gary C. King (New York: St. Martin's, 2001)

4. The Mountains

Mountains (General)
Lies, Legends & Lore of the San Juans by Roger Henn (Ouray, CO: Western Reflections, 1999)

Snippy the Horse and the San Luis Valley
Enter the Valley by Christopher O'Brien (New York: St. Martin's, 1999)
The Mysterious Valley by Christopher O'Brien (New York: St. Martin's, 1996)

Ted Bundy
The Stranger Beside Me by Ann Rule (New York: Signet, 1980)

Prisons, Old and New
This Is the Prison by Colorado Territorial Prison Museum (Cañon City, CO: Self-Published, 1993)
Museum of Colorado Prisons Self-Guided Tour by Museum of Colorado Prisons (Cañon City, CO: Self-Published)

Bob Ford
Colorado Gunsmoke by Ken Jessen (Loveland, CO: J. V. Publications, 1986)

Cripple Creek (General)
Cripple Creek: A Quick History by Leland Feitz (Colorado Springs, CO: Little London Press, 1967)
Cripple Creek Conflagrations by Lester L. Williams (Palmer Lake, CO: Filter Press, 1994)

The Old Homestead and Colorado Brothels
Six Racy Madams of Colorado by Caroline Bancroft (Boulder, CO: Johnson Books, 1965)
Meyers Avenue: A Quick History of Leadville's Red-Light District by Leland Feitz (Colorado Springs, CO: Little London Press, 1967)

The Baldpate Inn Key Room
The Baldpate Collections, Third Edition by The Baldpate Inn (Estes Park, CO: The Baldpate Inn, 2000)

Georgetown (General)
Georgetown: A Quick History by Kenneth Jessen (Loveland, CO: J. V. Publications, 1996)

Alferd Packer
Alferd Packer's Wilderness Cookbook by James E. Banks (Palmer Lake, CO: Filter Press, 1998)

Lone Survivor by Ken Hodgson (New York: Pinnacle Western, 2001)

Alferd G. Packer—Cannibal! Victim? by Ervan F. Kushner (Frederick, CO: Platte 'N Press, 1980)

Al Packer: A Colorado Cannibal by Jo Mazzula (F&J Mazzula, Date Unknown)

Alferd Packer's High Protein Gourmet Cookbook by Wendy & Kimberly Spurr (Grand Junction, CO: Centennial Publications, 1995)

Alferd Packer: Fact, Legend, Myth by Dr. James Starrs (Lake City, CO: Silver World Publishing, Co., 1997)

Leadville (General)
Leadville's Tales from the Old Timers, Book 1 by Helen Skala and Dora Krocesky (Leadville, CO: Self-Published, 1972)

Leadville's Tales from the Old Timers, Book 2 by Helen Skala (Leadville, CO: Self-Published, 1977)

Horace, Augusta, and Baby Doe Tabor
Silver Queen by Caroline Bancroft (Boulder, CO: Johnson Books, 1955)

The Legend of Baby Doe by John Burke (Lincoln, NE: University of Nebraska Press, 1974)

The Saga of H. A. W. Tabor by Rene L. Coquoz (Boulder, CO: Johnson Books, 1973)

The Tabor Opera House by Evelyn E. Livingston Furman (Leadville, CO: Self-Published, 1984)

Leadville Ice Palace
Palace of Ice by Edward Blair (Colorado Springs, CO: Little London Press, 1972)
King Pleasure Reigned in 1896 by Rene L. Coquoz (Boulder, CO: Johnson Books, 1969)

Colorado Mining
Climax by Stephen M. Voynick (Missoula, MT: Mountain Press Publishing Company, 1996)

Bishop Castle
"Castle Building" from My Point of View by James R. Bishop (Rye, CO: Self-Published, 2000)

The Penitentes
The Sacred World of the Penitentes by Alberto López Pulido (Washington, DC: Smithsonian Institution Press, 2000)

Telluride (General)
Telluride: A Quick History by Rose Weber (Colorado Springs, CO: Little London Press, 1974)

5. The Western Slope

Western Slope (General)
Beyond the Great Divide by Abbott Fay (Ouray, CO: Western Reflections, 1999)

Mesa Verde
The Wetherills of the Mesa Verde: Autobiography of Benjamin Alfred Wetherill by Maurine Fletcher, ed. (Lincoln, NE: University of Nebraska Press, 1987)

Durango & Silverton Narrow Gauge Railroad
Durango & Silverton Narrow Gauge Railroad: A Quick History by Duane A. Smith (Ouray, CO: Western Reflections, 1998)

Mike the Headless Chicken
The Official Mike the Headless Chicken Book by Teri Thomas (Fruita, CO: Fruita Times, 2000)

Glenwood Springs (General)
Glenwood Springs: A Quick History by Jim Nelson (Glenwood Springs, CO: Blue Chicken Publishing, 1998)

Doc Holliday
Doc Holliday, Bat Masterson & Wyatt Earp by E. Richard Churchill (Ouray, CO: Western Reflections, 1997)
John "Doc" Holliday: Colorado Trials and Triumphs by Emma Walling (Snowmass, CO: Self-Published, Date Unknown)

Hot Springs and Vapor Caves
Colorado's Hot Springs, Second Edition by Deborah Frazier George (Boulder, CO: Pruett Publishing Company, 2000)

INDEX BY CITY NAME

Cripple Creek
Cripple Creek & Victor Narrow Gauge Railroad, 180
Old Homestead, The, 123

Delta
Charles Kuralt, Accomplice to Herbicide, 174

Denver
B-1 Bomber (Wings Over the Rockies), 2
Behold, the Messiah!, 3
Birthplace of the Cheeseburger (Humpty Dumpty Drive-In), 10
Birthplace of the Denver Boot (Marugg Pattern Works), 10
Birthplace of Diagonal Crosswalks, 11
Birthplace of the Ice Cream Soda (Baur's Restaurant), 10
Birthplace of Shredded Wheat, 11
Birthplace of the VFW Post (John S. Stewart VFW Post #1 Museum), 10
Black American West Museum & Heritage Center, 4
Buckhorn Exchange, 5
Buffalo Bill Death Site, 7
Cheesman Park: Defiled Graveyard, 7
Denver Mint, 8
Denver Museum of Miniatures, Dolls, and Toys, 12
Forney Museum of Transportation, 13
If You Like Ike . . . , 13
JHB Button Museum, 15
Lakeside Amusement Park, 15
Mile High Step (State Capitol Building), 16
Murder of Alan Berg, The, 18
Neil Bush, Numskull, 19
Riverside Cemetery, 21
Roseanne's Big Break, 22
Talking Sidewalk, 23
Trailer Park Cowboy, 24
Unsinkable Molly Brown House, 25

Dinosaur
Dinosaur National Monument, 174
Dinosaur Town, 176

Drake

Durango

Empire

Englewood

Estes Park

Evergreen

Fairplay

Federal Heights

Flagler

Florence

Florissant

Fort Collins

Ice Palace Has Melted, The, 148
Michelange-no (St. Joseph's Church), 149
National Mining Hall of Fame and Museum, 150

Littleton
Alferd Packer's Grave, 34

Loma
Hangin' Time, 191

Longmont
Plan Fails, The, 66

Ludlow
Ludlow Massacre, The, 68

Mancos
Rain of Arrows, 193

Manassa
Jack Dempsey Museum, 151

Manitou Springs
Cave of the Winds, 102
Funky Arcades, 103
Manitou Cliff Dwellings Museum, 104

Meeker
End of the Junior Wild Bunch, The, 194
He Had It Coming . . . (Meeker Massacre), 194

Minturn
Holy Hills (Mount of the Holy Cross), 152

Monte Vista
Movie Manor, 154

Morrison
Ad Coors's Kidnapping Site, 35
Tiny Town, 36

Mosca
Colorado Alligator Farm, 155
Great Sand Dunes National Park, 156

Silver Cliff
Ghost Lights in the Cemetery, 164

Silver Plume
Griffin's Ghost, 165

Steamboat Springs
Slipping and Sliding (The Bridgestone Winter Driving School), 165

Sterling
Living Trees, The, 77

Strasburg
Real Golden Spike, The (Comanche Crossing Museum), 76

Trinidad
Ave Maria Shrine, 78

Vail
Captain Craig Button's Wild Ride, 166

Westminster
Traildust Steak House, 26

Woodland Park
Capture of the Texas 7, 105

INDEX BY Site Name